I SHALL NOT PASS THIS WAY AGAIN

AN AUTOBIOGRAPHICAL REFLECTION OF THE VARIED LIFE AND TIMES OF

ELBERT "BERT" RANSOM, JR.

CIVIL RIGHTS ACTIVIST, PREACHER, AND MUSICIAN

xulon
PRESS

Copyright © 2004 by Elbert Ransom, Jr.

I Shall Not Pass This Way Again
by Elbert Ransom, Jr.

Printed in the United States of America

ISBN 1-594675-25-2

All rights reserved solely by the author. The author guarantees all contents are original and do not infringe upon the legal rights of any other person or work. No part of this book may be reproduced in any form without the permission of the author. The views expressed in this book are not necessarily those of the publisher.

Bible quotations are taken from King James Version of the Bible. Copyright © 1976 by Thomas Nelson, Inc.

www.xulonpress.com

January 24, 2013

Bernard,

Read and get to know me better. You will be a great Rector.

Peace,
Bert

TABLE OF CONTENTS

Acknowledgements vii

Preface ix

Chapter I
    The Dawning of My Life 13

Chapter II
    Once Upon a Time In Alabama 21
    The Montgomery Bus Boycott 27

Chapter III
    In The Mississippi Valley 33

Chapter IV
    The Land Of Promise 41
        a. Victory In Spite of Odds 44
        b. The Children of Need 46
        c. Friends In The City 49
        d. Nonviolent Engagement 55

Chapter V
    New Horizons 61

Chapter VI
    Urban Renewal 67
    Transformation From Old to New 72

Chapter VII
    The Barry Years 75

Chapter VIII
    Called, Compelled and Committed 79

Chapter IX
    Go Ye Therefore 87

Chapter X
    Call to Community 97

Chapter XI
    In Search of Unity 103

Chapter XII
    Overcoming Rejection 107

Chapter XIII
    Fear in Times of Uncertainty 113

Chapter XIV
    Relentless Pursuit 117

Chapter XV
    Let the Church be the Church 121

Chapter XVI
    Race and Culture 131

Chapter XVII
    Continuing the Journey 137

Chapter XVIII
    Forever Hopeful 143

ACKNOWLEDGEMENTS

The nature of this book means the collection of a lot of data that had to be collaborated with many family members and longtime friends who played significant parts in my life's development. It has been a joy to remember the past with those who have vivid mental recollection of days gone by. I offer special thanks to God for my beloved parents, Elbert and Bernice Ransom whose positive insight into my future proved to be grounded in their relentless faith in God's unspeakable gifts. I thank my proofreaders, first my wife Louise who is attentive to details and given to fundamental sentence structure, my daughter Angela who was my first critical reader, my son Gregory for his historical analysis and review, and my stepson Stephen for his consistent encouragement and pride in my work. I am deeply in debt to my editor, Cindy Dyer who with her impeccable skills and patience assisted me in preparing the final transcript.

It was a blessing to locate my cardiologist, Dr. Benjamin Kaplan, of Chicago, Illinois, to assist me in recounting the constructive cardiac surgery that was performed on me by Dr. Lawrence Rubenstein in 1959. I am grateful for the longtime friendship of Herbert C. Jackson, Jr. who also assisted me in remembering our growing up together from ages six years old. It was Herbert's precocious mind at an early age that encouraged me to go beyond my reach.

My profound thanks to Melvin A. Mister, past Executive Director of the D.C. Redevelopment Land Agency, who gave me the opportunity to participate in the rebuilding effort of Washington,

D.C. during the urban renewal period of the 1970s, and believed that I could make a positive difference in the lives of indigent citizens. I am, of course highly appreciative of Brigadier General Donald J. Delandro, USA, (Ret.) and his wife Doretha for their generosity during some difficult times during our stay in Chicago. Thanks to the late Reverend Doctor Martin Luther King, Jr. for allowing me the treasured opportunity to participate in the great civil rights movement of the 1960s. This experience helped me to take advantage of the open door to the gospel ministry and I am richer in spirit for it.

I fully acknowledge and thank the members of the Alfred Street Baptist Church for their spiritual encouragement in my ministry. Their love and support has meant more to me than I can ever express. The thoughts of my mentors, Frank Davis and Sister Mary Elise will forever remain in my heart, as they worked like potters molding my life. I am grateful to the many people who crossed my path and left me the richer, because of their friendship and support.

PREFACE

The divine art of God's human creation appears to be a continuous study of complexities. The human specie is capable of adapting to an ever-changing environment on life's developmental pathway. Man has the ability to love, hate, deceive, commit acts of violence or harbor and plant seeds of peace. We are endowed with dual natures, which constitute the spiritual and creature comforts by which we live. Spirituality is expressed by our morals and religion, while the creature comforts are expressed in houses that we own, the clothes we wear, the wealth we amass, and the friends we acquire.

Throughout time, man has ventured unexplored territory, studying his biological makeup to improve medical technology, and even exploring human cloning. With the unfolding of the world order, man has been quite successful at improving and prolonging human life. While scientific knowledge moves toward its zenith, there remains a clamor for the fundamental understanding of man's existence. According to the story of creation, as found in Genesis 2:18-23, it was God's intent that we form communion with one another in growing His Kingdom on earth.

A prolific 16th century poet by the name John Donne understood human relationships when he penned "No Man Is An Island entire of itself. Every man is a piece of the continent, a part of the main. Any man's death diminishes me, because I am involved in mankind…"[1]

The haunting question of man's purpose continues to ponder the minds of anthropologists in their quest for human limits. The development of scientific and medical technology gives credence to extended life. We were made to be in relationship with one another, and because of individual distinct characters, we attempt to alter the divine plan of creation and the community of humanity.

Life is a journey of victories and agonies, accompanied by a constant need for us to understand our plight. Man's total existence has need for communion with others. A life of solitude can be adverse to the order of human creation, thereby, rendering the intent of human socialization null and void.

It is rewarding to positively affect the lives of those who are encumbered with the adversities of life. To this point, my life has been enriched by multiple experiences with other personalities, some of whom will be highlighted in the following chapters. In the scheme of life, time is short at best, and to reach the fullness of our time we should venture to do all the good that we can do to enhance the gift of life.

In a very short time the Superintendent of the Seattle, Washington's Public School System, the late Major General John H. Stanford, U.S. Army (Ret.), completely inspired the positive transformation of the School System. His faith in the good of humanity transformed the education of the children. Prior to his tenure, the public school system was fraught with low-test scores, major gaps between minority and white students, and incidences of violence were on the rise. The city was fragmented over the issue of education.[2]

While serving as superintendent, John combined his morals, his military leadership training, and his dogged desire to achieve, and lead the school system to heights never before realized. Standardized test scores soared for every student group in every subject, and the gap between minority and white students scores closed. The number of violent incidents dropped to a ten-year low and the number of high school dropouts declined by eight percent. It was John who encouraged me to pursue higher education.

During a memorial service for General Stanford, a fellow clergyman—Reverend Doctor Samuel B. McKinney, pastor emeritus, Mount Zion Baptist Church Seattle, Washington— said of him: "I have only just a minute, only sixty seconds in it, I didn't seek it, and I didn't choose it. But it is up to me to use it, suffer if I lose it, give account if I abuse it. I have just a tiny minute but eternity is in it." John used his time well.

I did not seek the precious gift of life. It is, indeed, a divine gift with no promise of longevity or return after death. It is a mystery at best, therefore, it is my duty to do all the good that I can, while I can, and with no regrets. I shall not pass this way again.

We have the option to use whatever time we are given in an accountable manner. Life can be an empty vessel or full of worthwhile attributes of loving, sharing, giving, comforting and learning. It is my belief that we are encumbered by God with will and desire, depending on our path and direction in life, and the goals we set for ourselves. In the scope of our living, time is of the essence. The question that is ever before us is: What will we do with the time that is given us? Every path that I have traveled—and each life that I encountered along the way—has enriched my life with more to give.

The world is pregnant with opportunities for us to take strides down the Jericho Roads of life looking for a chance to act out our Samaritan nature. Quite often, selfishness and greed become the basis for the many decisions that insulate us from the community of humanity. The experience of living on the sunny side of life is not the fortune of many that we encounter. We who understand the value of undeserved gifts of divine order have much to give, and little expectations of earthly gain. Giving freely brings balance in abundance to life. It is that aspect of humanity that is of God and His endless reserve of resources. Those who give unselfishly, have more to give.

Many of my travels have taken me to remote and depressed corners of the world, where I have come face to face with inhumane deprivation and human neglect. I have seen humanity socially and spiritually ravished as if God forgot about them. I have traveled among the poorest of the poor in the Cantonese provinces of Southern China, and those who live and die in the rawness of nature in Papua New Guinea and Solomon Island, and lest I forget the dying children of the Favellas of Brazil, who steal to survive and find their food in the garbage dumpsters.

This book is designed to reveal the true essence of a loving God who allows you and me to act as extensions of His grace and mercy while we pass this way. My life is a full vessel of blessings that are not for me alone, but to give to the least of these, regardless of race, culture, color or creed. The opportunity is now mine, for I shall not pass this way again. Read and gain new insights into your purpose for living, and how the rich episodes in the development of my life continue to prepare me for the journey ahead. I am in process, and in a constant state of becoming. I am not there, yet.

Elbert Ransom, Jr.

CHAPTER I

THE DAWNING OF MY LIFE

I expect to pass through this world but once; any good thing therefore that I can do, or any kindness that I can show to any fellow creature. Let me do it now; let me not defer or neglect it, for I shall not pass this way again.

Stephen Grellet

I was born in Jackson, Mississippi, in Hinds County in 1936. Jackson is the state capital of Mississippi, where a sordid history of harsh racial segregation against Black Americans has contributed to its infamous geographic profile. In 1916 -20 and 1928-32, Mississippi twice elected Theodore Gilmore Bilbo to the Governor's seat. He gained popularity because of his demagogic insistence on White supremacy. Bilbo died in 1947, while Congress was investigating charges that he had disqualified himself for the Senate by using intimidation tactics to keep Black Americans from voting.[1]

Mississippi has a dark history of the cruel and murderous treatment of black Americans. In 1955 Emmitt Louis Till, a fourteen year old black American male from Chicago, Illinois was brutally beaten and drowned in the Tallahatchie River by two white men. He was murdered for allegedly whistling to a white woman. I have a harsh memory of a story that my grandmother told me of a cruel and vicious incident that happened when she was a young girl in Forrest, Mississippi. She recounted that she and her family witnessed the burning of their house by the Ku Klux Klan, while they hid in the tall brush nearby. There are countless other murderous atrocities that have been committed in the state of Mississippi, because of hate: Medgar Evers, shot, 1963; James Earl Chaney, Andrew Goodman, Michael Schwerner, beaten and shot, 1964; and Vernon Dahmer, Sr., firebombing, 1966; Martin Wales, hanged, 1982; Revlia Epps, hanged, 1988; David Scott Campbell, hanged, 1990; and Andre Lamon Jones, hanged, 1992

The late Medgar Evers was a cousin of mine. He impressed and encouraged me to get involved in the Civil Rights Movement. Medgar was the first field secretary for the NAACP. He led a successful boycott against the Jackson, Mississippi merchants in the early 1960s, and attracted national attention. His efforts to have James Meredith admitted to the University of Mississippi in 1962 brought federal assistance which he had requested. Meredith was admitted to Ole Miss, where Evers was denied admission in the Law School. On June 12, 1963, as he was returning home, he was killed by an assassin's bullet. His legacy is present everywhere in Mississippi.[2]

Mississippi, once popularly known as "the land of the tree and the home of the grave," continues to be perceived as the state with a low degree of tolerance for racial harmony. Fear by black Americans, of ill willed Whites was common during my childhood in Mississippi, and many years thereafter. I can remember a time that my father rode me on his bicycle through a commercial section of Jackson. As we were approaching a white man, my father whispered to me, jokingly,"say hi peck." When we got close enough for the man to hear me, I said exactly what my father told me. For fear that the man heard me, my father shook with fear. Jackson was a bastion for violent segregationist activities against black Americans. Public accommodations were separate, unequaled and substandard. There were separate public water fountains, one for whites and one for coloreds. Black American men and women were not regarded as intelligent adults, no matter what educational level had been attained. Instead, they were often referred to as boy and girl, and when they grew to old age, and they were addressed as aunt and uncle.

Most of Jackson's black American population was employed as domestics and laborers, while their children attended inferior schools. My father did odd jobs as his major source of employment. He worked as a houseboy for an upper income white family washing their cars, scrubbing floors, cutting grass, shining shoes and running errands. For these menial tasks, he was paid $8.00 per week. My mother went beyond my father's four years of school to finish two years of college at Tougaloo College, northwest of Jackson. She worked as a certified teacher in a rural county school, outside of the city of Jackson. Their combined income was hardly enough to support our small but growing family.

In 1940 my brother, William Harper was born and was named for my maternal grandfather. The increase of our family necessitated the need for more income. In 1941 my father commuted to Biloxi, Mississippi after having been hired as a laborer during the construction of Keesler Fields Air Base. The job in Biloxi provided more income. A family friend encouraged my parents to relocate to New Orleans, Louisiana, in 1942, where jobs and salaries were better. Our family relocated to New Orleans, and as we were settling, my mother gave birth to my sister Addie Bernice. My father was hired, once again as a laborer by a ship building company called Higgins Industries. Higgins was the designer and builder of the historic Landing Craft Vehicle Personnel Boat, (LCVP). The vehicle was used in hundreds of landings in North Africa, Europe and the Pacific for the United States military personnel. This was when World War II was fully engaged and plant production was relegated to the military industrial complex, and many jobs were created to support the war effort.

Our residential beginning in New Orleans was three different rooming houses, until my parents found a small rental house on South Liberty Street. Ironically, because of the ravages of segregation, we were far from being liberated. We lived in a dense black American section of the city. My memory of the house was the sound of rats racing between the roof and the ceiling of the house. We would use broom handles to tap the ceiling to chase them away, but nothing frightened them. The house was a shotgun row house connected to the next house by a thin common wall leaving very little privacy. There were two major landmarks that depicted our neighborhood, the city's garbage incinerator and a large graveyard for white burials only. Unlike white neighborhoods where the streets were asphalt or concrete, our street was covered with oyster shells, overlaid with melted black tar, and as the automobile tires rolled over it the appearance was an imitation of asphalt. I was unaware that I was living in a black deprived ghetto.

My first indelible memory of South Liberty Street was when I attempted to befriend a new playmate that turned out to be the neighborhood bully. His name was Willie Cain. I said hello to him over the fence, and he replied by spitting in my face. The next impression came when a neighbor told my parents of a neighborhood gang of young black American males who were walking along side of the graveyard on a summer night, and a lone elderly woman approached them in passing. They, for no known reason, taunted her and beat her to death, and threw her over the fence onto the graveyard. One of the gang members was inquisitive enough to scratch a match to see who the victim was, only to discover that it was the mother of one of them. We further learned that the bereaved son lost his mind in grief and guilt.

The third impression was the constant fear of the sparks of fire that took flight from the smokestacks of the garbage incinerator. The sparks were living conditions that we were subjected to without any demonstrated concern from city leaders.

New Orleans was a city of racial and cultural complexities, and because of the pronounced cultural diversity, racial segregation remains a mystery. The irony is that many black and white persons are related by blood but with differences in skin color, hair texture, and manner of speaking find themselves totally apart, because of physical differences. The suffering that accompanies segregation sometimes pushes one to the brink of a " passé blanc" (passing for white) attitude. Many of my schoolmates resembled white persons, and pretended to be white.

I entered the Thomy Lafon Elementary School in 1942 when I was 6 years old. The school was a complex of small buildings, which were situated on an island in a sea of public housing units. Lafon was a typical neglected southern black American public school with a dedicated faculty committed to student achievement in spite of deprivation. Our textbooks were passed on to us after white students had used them. Because of the strict discipline of the teachers, there were times I thought they were horrible and unfeeling. However, I eventually learned that they did treasure us as future leaders and educators who needed strict guidance in support of our development. We were constantly reminded that the best was expected of us, as was emphasized in our school Alma Mater:

> *"Dear Lafon we love thee, more and more each day, and we'll try to please thee in most every way. When we're put to task dear. We shall never fail, by our efforts Dear Lafon, we will lift thee high."*

Thomy Lafon is where, early in my life, I was introduced to classical literature and music, as well as the rudiments of academia. This was a period of my life when I was encouraged by my mother to put forth my theatrical talents and participate in the annual Spring Festivals. These were opportunities for me to build on my earlier exposure before an audience when I sang my first solo, "God Bless America," at the school where my mother taught in Mississippi. My participation in the Spring Festivals set me on a life course of self-confidence and high self-esteem. I will be ever grateful to my mother, and my elementary school teachers who started me on my way to bigger stages of entertainment. Professor Victor attempted to teach me how to play the trumpet and clarinet, Bernice Durden Franklin, traveled to New York city each summer to see Broadway musicals, and returned to school with new ideas for different acts to be included in the Spring Festivals, and Peter Clark, my physical education teacher insisted that students learn how to develop themselves physically. Little did I know this was a period in my development that would prepare me for undertakings in my future public life.

When I entered the seventh grade, my parents saved $700.00 for the purpose of going into the dry cleaning business. It was a small neighborhood establishment for the cleaning and pressing of clothes. Because help was always needed, and with no money to hire additional persons, I was drafted by my parents to work as a helper.

This, of course, afforded me little or no time to enjoy my adolescent years, because of my confinement to the "shop," as it was called. I was expected to report to the shop, immediately, after school, while other boys my age were learning to play baseball and other sport activities. I felt deprived of my freedom; however, I was always surrounded by well meaning adults who had a great impetus on my continuing development. The shop became a social neighborhood institution. It was reminiscent of the traditional barbershop, where many people gathered and exchanged greetings, and gave and received pertinent community information, even if it was gossip.

The shop was in close proximity to the New Zion Baptist Church, where my religious training began. The church, in those days, was the center of our community; it was a place where one could get assistance in social, legal, and family matters. Our pastor, Reverend Abraham Lincoln Davis, Jr. was well connected in the political machinery of the city of New Orleans. He could, also, deliver the black vote in significant elections, which provided him political clout where necessary. The black Church has always appeared to be a mystery in the eyes of the white community, because it served as the center of the black Community. It was the place where most needs were met and resolved.

In the spring of 1950, I was graduated from Lafon and entered Walter L. Cohen Senior High School in the fall. Cohen was converted from an all white elementary school to an all black school, which came about because of the increased enrollment of black students, and a segregated school system.

It was a three-story building located in a predominantly white neighborhood. Our presence was resented as we passed through the community. I spent four years at Cohen preparing for higher education without knowing whether my parents could afford college tuition. To my surprise, our family increased by an additional daughter in 1953, named Josie Laverne. As a teen-ager, I suffered a bit of embarrassment when coming to the realization that my parents were still engaged in child bearing. However, Josie's arrival drew our little family closer together, and I became the doting big brother. Again, it was the love of my parents that gave me stability in my growing up, and accepting life as it unfolded. Cohen was where I developed a deep appreciation for the performing arts, and was introduced to singing grand opera. My first opera aria was Il Balen Del Suo Sorriso, from Verdi's *"Il Trovatore."* This musical art form propelled me into more serious study. I learned the vocal techniques of operatic singing, which caught the attention of prominent voice coaches who prepared me for what was thought to be a promising music career. New Orleans was a true mecca for aspiring instrumental and vocal musicians, and my heart was set on making a success in vocal music. I was involved in several local operatic presentations, and received positive noteworthy acclaim. My short-range intent was to position myself to receive a music scholarship from a college that had an outstanding music department.

CHAPTER II

ONCE UPON A TIME IN ALABAMA

⋄⇒◯⇐⋄

I was anxious to go to college away from New Orleans. Students, who were ahead of me in colleges that were miles away, strongly motivated me to go away. I had this yearning to travel back and forth to some campus far away. Graduation from Cohen was in 1954, and my wishes came true. I was offered music scholarships to Dillard, Southern, Xavier Universities, and Alabama State College for Negroes, currently Alabama State University. I immediately chose Alabama State. In retrospect, I elected to attend this university in an effort to travel as far away from my parents' dry cleaning establishment as possible. It was time to enter the real world of growing toward manhood. My parents helped me prepare for the beginning of my college career, as we shopped at Sears and Roebuck Department Store for a trunk, suitcase, and a pair of buckskin shoes with red soles. After all, I was becoming a college man.

I departed New Orleans for Montgomery during July. Instead of waiting for the beginning of the fall session, I went in the summer to begin my work scholarship to earn enough credits. This was to be my first long trip from home alone. My parents did not have the train fares to accompany me to the campus. I boarded the Louiseville-Nashville train, called the "Hummin Bird". With my trunk, suitcase and a cardboard shoebox containing my mother's southern fried chicken and homemade pound cake. I was off from the swampy marshlands of Louisiana to the red clay hills of Alabama. As the train traveled past the backyards and farmlands of the tiny rural townships and cities from New Orleans to Montgomery passengers disembarked and boarded at each stop. Many were headed north in search of a new life that would give them more than the farmlands offered. The conductor directed them to the car according to race, as I had been when I boarded the train in New Orleans. The black passengers traveled with food because the train's dining car was reserved for White's only. Separate waiting rooms in the station, separate riding accommodations, the lack of a comfortable eating area for black passengers became a serious concern for me. The authorities called it separate but equal, but equality was never intended for persons of my hue. I traveled with the shadow of fear and insult with nowhere to complain.

After arriving in Montgomery in the late afternoon, I took a local taxi to the campus and saw the city for the first time. The land was hilly, as compared to the flat land of Louisiana. I was now in what was called the cradle of the confederacy, where in 1865 Jefferson Davis took the oath on the steps of the Alabama state capitol building to serve as provisional president of the Confederate States.

I began to realize the true beauty of Montgomery as I passed antebellum mansions surrounded by the arresting beauty of magnolia trees and pretty flowers. I was now in a new environment open for exploration for the next four years. After arriving on the campus, I reported to the finance office and met the bursar who provided my meal tickets, assigned me a dormitory, and a job in the music building, My dormitory had the appearance of a World War II wooden army barrack in need of much repair, and housed a small number of students who were attending summer school. The building was depressing, dimly lit, and reeked of sweat and a combination of urine and after-shave lotion. There was no floor covering nor was there paint on the walls. I found my stark room furnished with three double deck bunks, a desk and a chair. This was hardly a place conducive to study. I met a student in the bathroom who appeared discouraged and unhappy. He was the unofficial committee of one who welcomed me to the campus.

His first words to me were, "Did you just arrive?" I answered, "yes!" He said to me, "Don't unpack, because you won't like it here- I despise this place." I thought to myself, "what a greeting". Could Alabama State College be as bad as the student had intimated? I then found my room and entered, finding three double decked sleeping bunks, which appeared to be overcrowded for the small room size. Later, I met five of my new roommates who appeared and claimed their space. After a few days on campus, these roommates became my dearest friends and brothers. They were chiefly responsible for helping me adjust to the college environment. I met many other students who would become longtime acquaintances and friends.

Dr. Frederick Douglas Hall, chairman of the music department, met me in his office for a verbal orientation and vocal audition. I sang William Dawson's, *"Jesus Walked This Lonesome Valley"*, and the *Toreador Aria* from George Bizet's opera Carmen. I was accepted in the college concert choir. I was elated for the acceptance, because I later learned that freshmen students were not normally accepted until their second year in school. My voice teacher, Robert E. Williams, was a Morehouse College graduate and did graduate work at Columbia University in New York. He was anxious for me to begin my study with him and develop a strong repertoire of songs. He was also eager for me to meet a former Morehouse classmate of his who was also new to Montgomery. This friend had come to serve as the new pastor of Dexter Avenue Baptist Church, which was a small church, located at the end of two city blocks of the state capitol buildings. Williams finally introduced me to his friend. Who was The Reverend Doctor Martin Luther King, Jr. King and I became friends. Shortly thereafter I joined Dexter Avenue Baptist Church, and became a member of the church's sanctuary choir where I was often featured as a soloist.

King loved visiting the campus, and felt very much at home when he was there. He had flirted with the idea of becoming a college professor, however, that never came about though he did serve as a visiting lecturer when called upon. When he and his wife, Coretta, needed help at the parsonage to do yard work, mop and wax floors, and baby- sat Yolanda, their first child, I was asked to assist them. I performed these tasks each Saturday morning for a small fee. For a struggling college student, the opportunity to earn a few dollars was appreciated. They were quite supportive of my efforts in furthering my education; the menial job helped me meet some basic needs. They were ardent music lovers, and Coretta and I, often sang duets together in the church choir.

As King's life became busier, I spent many days traveling around Montgomery as his companion, as he went about his meetings, errands and church work. I especially enjoyed the times we stopped for a hearty southern lunch of collard greens, sweet potatoes, macaroni and cheese, fried chicken, corn bread, and bread pudding for dessert. King loved to eat, and so did I. It was much better than the food in the college dining hall. I deeply cherished the close friendship we shared during those early days.

Dexter Avenue Baptist Church was a small congregation of approximately three hundred of Montgomery's most influential and respected black citizens, and many of them had respectable incomes. Education was a tradition at Dexter, as the ministers before King were well trained and shared their knowledge freely.

The congregation was accustomed to an active social gospel from the days of Vernon Johns, who was one of King's predecessors.[1] It was ironic that the church building was situated on a corner in a square of the Alabama State Government's enclave of office buildings, with the state capitol building majestically resting on a mound of land at the apex of the square. Each Sunday when Dexter's worship ended we would say our good-byes on the front steps of the church under the shadow of the capitol dome. The irony continues, in that, out of this little church came a civil rights movement that challenged the segregationist policies and practices in America. As we worshipped, life continued in Montgomery under its diabolical system of segregation.

In spite of segregation, the faculty of Alabama State College was dedicated to training future black educators, who were the children of share croppers, domestics, and laborers, to make meaningful contributions to the underprivileged population. The college was completely black American, but because of the excellent clay tennis courts, white students from nearby colleges would come to play on our courts. We were not allowed to play on theirs.

Montgomery was a clean and orderly city, but under closer scrutiny, it was two cities, one for whites and one for blacks. In his book, *Stride Toward Freedom,* King provided some pertinent statistics about life and resources in Montgomery during the 1950s.[2] He described it as a prominent market for cotton, livestock, yellow pine, and hardwood lumber, and one of the nation's centers for commercial fertilizer. Montgomery was not an industrial city, and the lack of industry gave rise to the number of black persons who worked as domestics and laborers. There was a disparaging gap of housing conditions between white and black people. Overall, relationships were falsely polite, at best. The scene was set for something adversely major to happen in race relations. Montgomery was a powder keg with a short fuse that was being ignited by poor treatment of blacks by whites. Tensions mounted in every aspect of public accommodations.

During the Christmas break of 1954, I traveled back to New Orleans to visit my family for the holidays. After a two-week stay, I returned to Montgomery on a train that arrived late in the morning causing me to be late for an early class. I decided to leave my luggage at the station and claim it later in the evening. I returned to the station with my roommate, Virgil Hodges. Virgil was an unusual student at the college, he was from Atlanta, Georgia but he attended high school at Tilden in New Hampshire. His familiarity with white people was a normal way of life as opposed to most of us other students. Two shabbily dressed white policemen approached Virgil, as he was keeping an eye on my luggage. One of the policemen asked him, in a disrespectful gruff tone, "Is that your bag, boy?" Virgil answered with confidence, "It's for my man," as he gestured to me. The officer grew angry, I walked to where they were talking and asked, "Is there anything wrong, officer?" He looked at me with hatred in his eyes and said, "Nigger, where you from? "I answered, "New Orleans, Louisiana." He, then asked, "Did you jess git in heah?" I answered, No! His next words were," Nigger you might git away wid saying yes and no in New Orleans, but you in Montgomery, Alabama, You hear me?" As he spoke, his body shook with nervousness. I answered him, "yes sir." He then ordered me to open my suitcase, as he pulled his gun and pointed it at me. His partner shined his flashlight into the suitcase, and said, "dat ain't hit!" The pair returned to their cruiser and left in a huff. I was terribly frightened, and quickly realized that two racist, illiterate and untrained policemen who saw me as anything but human could have killed me. I felt dehumanized and degraded. This event happened because of my black skin, and good grammar. I looked toward the black waiting room for support, only to find it filled with people who stared in fear of the police.

    I hastened to contact my pastor, Martin Luther King, Jr. the next day, and recounted the horrible incident to him in hopes of gaining support, by way of a formal complaint. King listened to me politely without making comment, which caused me to feel defeated. I learned from some local people that the policeman who publicly degraded me was widely known throughout the black Community as Shaky. He had a physical condition that caused him to violently shake when he was upset. He enjoyed the reputation of keeping the black community in line with the administration of brutality. After the train station episode, I became very conscious of the depth of the racial divide in Montgomery.

    During the spring of 1955, the late U.S. Congressman Adam Clayton Powell visited Montgomery, and was denied the right to speak in the City's Civic Center. He was first given the right to use the center, but because of his strong public stand against segregation, he was later denied use. It was blatantly clear that Montgomery's city fathers were exercising their racist practices, because Powell was black.[3] It opened my eyes, to the extent that hate could go. As the time of the program neared, organizers hurriedly looked for an alternate location. There was no church or school auditorium large enough to accommodate a large audience. The Alabama State College gymnasium seemed to be most appropriate for the gathering, and it was agreed that the event would be held at the college. Powell arrived exuding flamboyance, self-assurance and cockiness. I sat in the bleachers of the gym, sitting above floor level. I observed Martin Luther King, Jr., and Coretta seated, and giving full attention to the speaker. During this period of his life, King's civil rights contributions were his solicitation of NAACP funds and the delivery of social gospel homilies on Sunday mornings at Dexter. One of the most memorable sermons he preached when anxiety between the races had reached a hiatus was, *"When Peace Becomes Obnoxious."* He was no doubt referring to the strange hush of the stagnant life of the two races of people residing in Montgomery, separate and unequal. We were living under an unreal peace that was on the brink of exploding. It became obvious that this false peace existed when Rosa Parks, a black American woman sat down in a vacant seat on the Cleveland Avenue bus. The seat was reserved for white patrons only. When ordered to move by the driver of the bus, she refused. The driver had her arrested, which got the attention of the black citizens of Montgomery. As someone familiar with the treatment of black people on the bus, I frequently rode the Cleveland Avenue bus to travel back and forth from the campus to other sections of the city. Often, in compliance with the social mores, I paid my fare at the front of the bus, and was often ordered by the driver to step down and board by using the back door. This prevented black passengers from walking through the white section of the bus. Sometimes, while walking to the rear door, the driver would drive off leaving me at the bus stop. I thought this was most cruel, especially, when I didn't have another fare for the next bus. On occasions, I would have to walk and cry. The pain of being hated hurt so very deeply.

THE MONTGOMERY BUS BOYCOTT

Segregation of races was the law and a way of life in the United States. Montgomery, Alabama was among the leading cities with a demonstrative practice of racial divide. Since Jefferson Davis took the oath for the provisional presidency of the confederate states, the system had not experienced national attention for its racial bitterness. On December 1, 1955, a black seamstress, Rosa Parks, climbed aboard the Cleveland Avenue bus to return to her home after a days work at Montgomery Fair, one of the notable department stores in downtown Montgomery. On this infamous day the Montgomery Police bringing world attention to America's shame arrested Rosa Parks. When she sat in the first seat behind the seating plan that was reserved for whites only, black people in Montgomery stood up for justice. Enough was enough, and within minutes the word went through the black community that Rosa

Parks had been arrested. To many white people in Montgomery, Rosa Parks had broken the law and had gotten what she deserved. For the black community, the opportunity for justice had come and had to be addressed. The students of Alabama State rejoiced at the opportunity for a show down, and hopefully, an end to segregation.

The organization of the response to the arrest was spontaneous. E. D. Nixon, who headed a local community organization known as the Progressive Democrats, moved with great haste to sign the bond to release Rosa Parks. On Friday, December 2, Nixon informed King about the arrest the evening before. He strongly suggested that a bus boycott was in order. He felt that only a boycott would communicate to white folks that segregation is painful. By denying them bus fares; it was possible that something would be done. If the majority of blacks stayed off the bus, the financial repercussions would make the boycott a success. Seventy-five percent of the bus company's patrons were black. King agreed that the boycott would be an effective method to get the attention we desperately needed. King, Ralph Abernathy a young local pastor of the First Baptist Church and Nixon discussed the exciting advantages of a boycott. They needed to sell the idea to the black community. During these delicate times of early organizing, fear for King's safety was a concern for Coretta and others who were acquainted with covert terror in the south.

Following proper and respected protocol, King, Abernathy, and Nixon contacted Reverend H.H. Hubbard, president of the Montgomery Baptist Ministers Alliance to solicit his support. This was a necessary contact to make, because the Alliance was respected by all of the black ministers in Montgomery, and to bypass the president could have meant immediate failure. Every black Baptist Minister was called by King, Abernathy and Nixon and apprised of the intent to boycott. The Methodist ministers were informed as a group as they were attending a denominational conference at one location. An initial organizational meeting, consisting of ministers and civic leaders was held at the Dexter Avenue Baptist Church. The result of the meeting was unanimous agreement to boycott the bus company.

A new day had come to Montgomery where the determination

to overcome the barriers of segregation was finally at hand. Fear of the system, particularly jail and death, was no longer a deterrent to forging ahead for justice. Informational leaflets were disseminated, spelling a plea for every black person and white sympathizer to refrain from riding the bus.

> **DON'T RIDE THE BUS TO WORK, TO TOWN, TO SCHOOL, OR ANY PLACE MONDAY, DECEMBER 5. ANOTHER NEGRO WOMAN HAS BEEN ARRESTED AND PUT IN JAIL BECAUSE SHE REFUSED TO GIVE UP HER SEAT. DON'T RIDE THE BUSES TO WORK, TO TOWN, TO SCHOOL, OR ANYWHERE ON MONDAY. IF YOU WORK, TAKE A CAB, OR SHARE A RIDE, OR WALK. COME TO THE MASS MEETING, MONDAY AT 7:00 P.M. AT THE HOLT STREET BAPTIST CHURCH FOR FURTHER INSTRUCTIONS.**

The boycott began on Monday, December 5, as planned. One observer reported that the buses rolled out of the bus barn at 6:00 a.m. and no black person boarded along the route. Along with other students, I arose early to stand on the corner of Jackson and Thurman Streets to see for our-selves if Black persons would stick together in what proved to be the most dramatic effort in community empowerment that the south had ever experienced.

It was during the period of my youthful life that I found hope for the future. In addition to accompanying King on trips around the city, I also served as a bus boycott student organizer, asking students at the college to stay off the buses. I also informed them of mass meetings and assisted in the preparation and distribution of informational flyers. Montgomery's black community exuded an aura of confidence and a do- or -die spirit. By accident, I was caught up in the making of history. It was a transformation of life from social bondage to freedom.

Because the start of the boycott was such a mammoth success, there was a need to organize for future efforts. The decision was

I Shall Not Pass This Way Again

made to continue the boycott until conditions were met. It was the idea of Abernathy, Nixon and the Reverend Earl French, minister of the Hilliard Chapel A.M.E. Zion Church to form an organization that would be recognized and charged with the responsibility of acting in behalf of the black community. The Montgomery Improvement Association, MIA- was formed, with King nominated as president. The success of the first day of the boycott gave impetus to the community. It demonstrated what the oppressed could do when there is a united effort. This was a day that showed that wearisome souls are granted strength and determination when Divine Order becomes evident. There was something unusual about the behavior of the boycott participants that engendered courage instead of defeat. In spite of the forces of evil attempting to impede the progress that was being made, there appeared to be a moral force at work ensuring victory.

The MIA provided guidance for the boycott that brought about the application of passive resistance. King knew from history that violence taken against the system was a useless cause. In 1831 Nat Turner, a black slave from Southampton County, Virginia, killed his slave master and his entire family as they lay sleeping. Turner and his force of forty slaves continued their rampage, killing all of the white people they encountered. He was, eventually captured and put to death. King and the MIA's approach was to overcome the oppressor with a moral state of mind, thereby bringing about peaceful coexistence. This brand of resistance was viewed by many as paradoxical in nature but with patience it was sure to succeed in due time.

After many days of tired feet, mass meetings, arrests, and disappointments, the boycott persevered. It lasted one year, and ended in total victory. On Tuesday, November 13, 1956, the U. S. Supreme Court handed down a decision that declared Alabama's state and local laws unconstitutional regarding segregated buses. I can now look back in retrospect and say that I took part in the dramatic struggle of 50,000 black people as we used patience, a spirit of love, and our tramping feet to bring about justice in the cradle of the confederacy. The Montgomery bus boycott was a model of mass discipline, undergirded with determination to be victorious at any cost. As I reflect on those uncertain times when Montgomery's black people were wandering in a wilderness seething with hatred and interposition, I am reminded of the poignant words of the 19th century poet James Russell Lowell:

> *Truth forever on the scaffold, wrong forever on the throne*
> *Yet that scaffold sways the future, and behind the dim unknown,*
> *Standeth God within the shadow, keeping watch above his own.*

CHAPTER III

IN THE MISSISSIPPI VALLEY

*In the Mississippi Valley, in the crescent bend
stands our loved and noble Xavier, for her praises send.
Wave her colors, bear them onward gold and white so
true; hail to thee all hail dear Xavier! Hail, all Hail XU.*
                                                    Annie Lisle

I am a firm believer that wherever we have been, wherever we are, and wherever we shall go is a reflection of Divine Order. With our mortal limitations, it is impossible to be in complete charge of our destiny. There are times when we organize plans for stages of our lives that appear to be finite until some unexpected event causes an interruption and a change in the flow of the plan.

I began my college career at Alabama State College for Negroes in the summer of 1954. My intent was to complete four years of study as a music major specializing vocal supervision. During the spring of the second year, I received a letter from my mother informing me that Frank Davis was on a musical tour in New Orleans with Fred Waring and the Pennsylvanians. She wrote that Frank had asked for me, only to be told that I was enrolled in Alabama State College. Frank was a close family friend and was also my mentor for many of my adolescent years. I admired him; he had all of the qualities to which I aspired. He was tall, handsome, affable and an unusual talented bass baritone singer and he was in high demand by appreciative audiences. Two years before I began college, Fred Waring contracted with him as the first and only Black singer in his show. His singing voice was unlike any bass baritone that I had ever heard, and the same was true for many others who had the privilege to hear him sing. He had the ability to sing three octaves. Before I began college, he spent an inordinate period of time as my voice coach. My ambition was to cultivate my voice to sing like Frank. When he learned that I had enrolled in Alabama State College, he asked my parents to contact me and arrange for a transfer to Xavier University in New Orleans, Louisiana. He explained to them that Xavier had a more advanced music department and that it would be a better showcase for my talents. He offered to speak to Sister Mary Elise, chairperson of Xavier's music department, in hopes of making the transfer orderly. I was not engaged in a challenging course of musical study at Alabama, nor was there a broad enough audience where talent could have been recognized for further development. I readily accepted the offer and completed my second year while the Montgomery bus boycott was in full force.

I left Alabama in June of 1956, with some regrets, because of my commitment to the bus boycott, Martin Luther King and his little family, and the many friends that I had come to know and love. I would miss singing with the Dexter Avenue Baptist Sanctuary choir and the beauty of this antebellum city. I said my good - byes to many classmates and to a temporary lifestyle that proved to me that even strangers could invade each other's lives and richly enhance one another.

I arrived in New Orleans with the intention of entering Xavier University. I had some apprehensions because I felt that Xavier's scholastic standards were somewhat out of reach for me. I had not applied myself to studies in Alabama. I spent more time singing and trying to develop myself socially, which is another way to say that I frittered my time away on less important matters. Now I was entering a realm of serious commitment and study. The day for new student registration arrived and I was concerned about student financial aid. My parents were not able to pay the full tuition that was required for each semester. Sister Elise had promised financial assistance upon registration, but apparently the bursar did not honor her commitment, and I was turned away. Registration was overseen by the university registrar, Sister Miriam Frances, who informed me that there was no student aid for me and suggested that if I had no money to register, I should find a job and come back when I had enough money. I responded that I did not know where I could find a job, and her reply was, "There's construction work." I was devastated and disappointed. I was between two schools; the one that I left and the other that would not accept me because of the unwillingness to provide me with some degree of financial assistance. I reported my dilemma to Sister Elise and her comforting words provided me some assurance born out of patience. She assured me that if my parents could borrow money for one semester, financial assistance would be available to me for the duration of my study at Xavier. I told my parents and in their normal supportive manner they assured me that they would do all they could. We searched until we found a viable college assistance program called the Tuition Plan that was reasonable and manageable enough for our meager family budget. The strong support of Sister Elise and my family sustained me through this trying time. There were other memorable supportive measures in my efforts to gain acceptance into Xavier. My mother's prayers and continuing faith in God as we made nine-day novenas in search of rich blessings. I shall never forget the unsolicited financial contributions from my younger brother William, who gave me his earnings from his newspaper delivery job. I barely had enough money to enter the fall session of 1956; however, I completed the first semester with passable grades and earned the respect of my teachers while regaining my self-esteem. Sister Elise arranged financial assistance for me, as she had promised, and for that I shall be eternally grateful.

I began my studies with a degree of anxiety hoping that I would do well in the days ahead. The two years at Alabama State were not a lost cause, because I gained a deeper insight into the cruelties of racial prejudice and its adverse affect on human destiny, I was ready to prepare myself for the future. While Sister Frances discouraged me at registration, I was prepared to persevere from the lessons that I had learned from the Montgomery bus boycott. I was given a second chance to prove myself a dedicated student. I made a commitment to apply myself to the Xavier curriculum.

Xavier was quite different from Alabama State. It was solidly religious and administered by 72 catholic nuns of the Order of the Sisters of the Blessed Sacrament. Their lives were dedicated to the education, spiritual, and moral development of Negro and Native American students in the South, where opportunities were nonexistent if you were not White. Catholic mass was part of the general order of the day and prayers were observed before and after each class. The faculty of nuns was augmented by laypersons and Catholic priests. The campus atmosphere was quiet and reverently acknowledged the presence of the Holy Eucharist. Although I was not Catholic, I served as a Eucharistic guard. I lived with my parents, and they often reminded me of my purpose as a student. My goal was to become a leading opera performer, by studying under accomplished musicians who taught me the art of singing and acting.

Living in New Orleans can be a dejecting experience for dark-skinned black Americans. Two groups can reject you: white people and fair- skinned black people. It remains a city where fair- skinned black people appear to have more privileges than those of blacker hues, and in many situations their behavior has demonstrated an isolationist attitude. Fair- skinned black persons often lived in communities of their kind such as the seventh ward of the city and other neighborhoods of light skinned concentration. Xavier University was a scholastic haven for many light-skinned black persons. Often, light and black skinned students interacted on the campus but off campus was a different world where integration among students was noticeably absent. I recall seeing many light-skinned Xavier students riding the public bus sitting in the section reserved for whites only.

As a black- skinned student, my anxieties about Xavier were not restricted to academics and the lack of tuition. I was also quite concerned about my social development in an institution that was deeply reflective of the New Orleans culture. Within the black culture there were two communities that openly practiced racist behavior. It was common to hear the words, "If you are light, you're alright; if you are brown, stick around; and if you are black, get back." Xavier's student population very clearly followed those lines of discrimination. In one example, I was invited to a social event at the home of a classmate who lived in a part of the city where light skinned black persons were prevalent. During the social I was left alone, except for the hospitality of the host. I was convinced that because I was an outsider to the neighborhood the other guests who were residents of the neighborhood did not welcome me. This was my first introduction to rejection within the Black race, because of the dark color of my skin. It became quite clear to me that though I was invited by a friend, I was completely out of place.

I became engaged in serious study and performance of grand opera. In 1925 Sister Elise, the founding director of Xavier's Opera Workshop, initiated the Opera Theatre and provided New Orleans with high quality performances of professional caliber. The New Orleans community was most appreciative and supportive of Xavier's Opera Workshop, which staged full-scale operas during the fall of each year. As a young boy, I admired and enjoyed the opera and could not wait to participate. When the time came, I took on the following roles: Operas—George Bizet, Carmen, El Dcairo; Charles Gounod, Faust, Valentine; Wolfgang Amadeus Motzart, The Marriage of Figaro, Dr. Bartello; Giuseppe Verdi, Rigoletto, Sparafucille; and Il Trovatatore, Conte di Luna. Musicals—Kurt Wield, Lost in the Stars, Reverend Stephen Kumalo; Gian-Carlo Menotti, The Medium, Mr. Gobineau and The Telephone, Ben.

These musical experiences in the performing arts prepared me for a broader arena beyond New Orleans and exposed me, at an early age, to racial and cultural integration before the mixing of the races became legal in the South. The faculty at Xavier was predominantly made up of white instructors and professors from the north and eastern seaboard of the United States and some from abroad. It became apparent why Frank Davis insisted that I attend Xavier, it gave me an opportunity for a more diverse and broader musical education.

Sister Elise will always have a place in my heart, because without her support and faith in my ability to succeed in music and my studies my college career would have been bleak. Her constant prayers and encouragement gave me the stamina that propelled me through times when all seemed to have been lost. I shall be ever grateful for the vision of Saint Katharine Drexel who saw possibilities in the plight of many descendants of former black slaves and Native Americans. She presented us with the prerequisites to go and compete for professional status in the American dream. As she became aware of the sufferings of Native Americans, and African American people in the South and the East, she extended her charity to them. Xavier University of Louisiana and the many proud graduates over the years stand as vivid testaments of Saint Katharine's benevolence and I am one of the proud products of her caring.[1] During my second year at Xavier, I became attracted to a young woman who also shared my love for music, and the attraction became mutual. We spent every waking minute together when we were not committed to class. Our relationship was such that we often spoke of marriage after college. As a token of commitment I remember giving her a silver dollar to keep as a first bank deposit after our marriage. She graduated one year before I did and her father and one of her brothers traveled to Xavier to attend her graduation ceremony. While they were visiting, my parents invited them to lunch in our home. When her father and brother departed, our relationship deteriorated. My family and I concluded that our meager standard of living was not acceptable to her family. After she returned to her home-town, she wrote a letter to me, and explained that her parents had great plans for her to go to Florence, Italy for further musical study. I never heard from her again. To say the least, I was devastated. The rejection that I received from her prepared me to face the realities of life, even when you see yourself, as others do not. I absorbed myself in music. Living in New Orleans I was constantly reminded of the harsh dual racial system that ordered my life day by day. There was no difference in the treatment of black people in New Orleans or Montgomery. Often, I would observe the many public freedoms of white people that were off limits to black people. There were times when I would pass attractive restaurants, movie theaters, amusement parks, and public schools where people of my race were not allowed to enter. As a young college student who saw in Montgomery what racial denial did to the psyche of black people, I grew strongly determined to be the best that I could be, and reject racial segregation as long as it existed.

While a student at Xavier University, my parents didn't have extra money for my immediate needs; therefore, I took a part time job as a domestic worker in the home of Felix Julius and Ruth Dreyfouse for $1.00 an hour. Mr. Dreyfouse was a prominent and respected architect in New Orleans and was responsible for the architectural design of the second addition to the Calliope Public Housing Projects for black people, which were constructed during the years 1952–1956. My family residence was located in the older buildings of the project.

My chores while employed by the Drefouses, were mopping, waxing and vacuuming their floors, shoe shining, gardening, washing their automobiles, serving dinner to the family one evening a week, and serving social parties on special occasions. The couple had one adult son, John Felix, who lived with them and was eight years my senior. John was spoiled and uncertain about his future. He had attempted an architectural degree at Tulane University; however, he was not successful to his father's chagrin. John decided to become a wholesale coffee salesman, and found his niche in sales. For a long time, I envied John in his white Ivy League demeanor, without a care in the world, and a resourceful family that he could depend on when times got tough. On Saturdays and Sundays he and his friends played tennis or went boating. They were free to do whatever they wanted to do without question of race. He gave his worn, broadcloth button down collar shirts to me, and my mother would be ever so grateful to turn the collars to the unworn side for me to wear.

It was important to me that John recognized me as an equal, but that seemed never to be the case. He was ensconced in his world of freedom and supremacy. That was a clear distinction of white and black people in the South. My desire to be recognized as an equal was very pronounced when my picture or name would appear in the city's newspaper as a reported success in an opera role at Xavier. However, I remained just their servant. Serving dinner to the family was an interesting dynamic in itself. Mrs. Dreyfouse sat at the head of the table, while Mr. Dreyfouse sat at the opposite end, and the family sat around them. Mrs. Dreyfouse activated a foot buzzer when courses of food were to be served or dishes removed, and at the sound of the buzzer, I came to accommodate the need. They insisted that I wear a white shirt, bow tie, black slacks, and a white servant's jacket to serve dinner. While they were of the southern tradition, they were not disrespectful. I learned that they didn't really need my services, but it was their way of making a positive contribution to a needy black person, and I was available. I was happy to learn many social graces from them that proved to be an asset later in my life.

CHAPTER IV

THE LAND OF PROMISE

During the early 1900s, many black Americans left the farmlands of the south and journeyed north to escape the oppressive conditions of inadequate employment, inferior education, social injustice, unwarranted arrests, and lynching. Industrial cities in the north offered factory jobs to black American workers who had no skills but a willingness to work. Friends and relatives who had already migrated northward sent messages of their success, and informed those remaining of the numerous opportunities that were available in the north. For sixty years, (1900-1960), the black American migration was at its height.

In 1959, at age 22, after graduating from Xavier, I became one of those statistics who relocated from the South to the North. Prior to my departure, I applied to the New Orleans Parish School System for a teaching certificate with hopes of being hired as a music teacher. The black community of New Orleans looked to black American schoolteachers as having attained a level of respect. The beginning salary at that time was $3,400 annually. I would have been satisfied with a teaching position until my aunt in Chicago, Illinois contacted me. She had migrated from Jackson, Mississippi to Chicago in 1945. She married an industrious man who was successful in several business ventures. They invited me to leave the south and seek a teaching position in Chicago. They also offered me lodging accommodations until I became economically secure.

I arranged to depart New Orleans in July of 1959, and traveled north for a full day into the night, going through Mississippi for most of the day and arriving in Tennessee in the late afternoon, across the Ohio River into southern Illinois. Along the railroad, the sites were rural countrysides and the backyards of small towns and distant cotton fields. The train made stops along the way to pick up passengers and to deliver milk, mail and other parcels. The station stops were architecturally generic with one large well-lighted room for white passengers and one small dimly lighted room for black passengers. This room was usually dirty and unkempt, filled with chattering sharecroppers who were on their way to the lands of promise, namely Chicago, Detroit, St. Louis or Gary, Indiana. They seemed uncertain about the transition to an unfamiliar setting; however, they were willing to chance the move from the oppressive treatment in the south. The room was usually policed by the local police and railroad conductors, both whom were always white men barking unfriendly orders. Positive changes in race relations between black and white Americans seemed remote and in the far distant future, if at all. The Montgomery bus boycott had called attention to black mistreatment in the south but the racial struggle was still alive and clearly evident. As I observed my fellow black passengers carrying their shoddy luggage bound with ropes and neck ties, their lunches from the kitchens of the shanties out of which they had come, I could not help but wonder if life would be any better in the North.

I arrived at Chicago's 12th Street Station late in the evening of July 3rd, and was met by my uncle and driven to a predominant black community on the south side where the ensuing years of my life began. Being in Chicago was an experience of becoming an insignificant part of a great mass of northern humanity. I was at the threshold of a new level of trials in becoming an independent adult. I was excited about the possibility of obtaining employment and undertaking my own responsibilities. I took the time to meet relatives, some that I did not know, and to become reacquainted with those I had known. During my early days in this new city, I was taken by my uncle on several exploratory tours to see the great expanse and make up of Chicago, including the downtown loop that hosts Chicago's financial, cultural, civic and tourist centers. I learned that the name "loop" originated from the path traced by the elevated train tracks in their encirclement of the downtown business center. I was taken to view the high cost residential condominiums on North Lakeshore Drive and the adjacent communities, which took up residence along Lake Michigan, such as Evanston, Glencoe, Wilmette, Winnetka, Glencoe, Glenview, and Highland Park. These communities were far from the residential sites that I had seen along the railroad tracks en-route to Chicago.

The Water Tower, which survived the historic fire of 1871, and the ingenuous results of the rebuilding efforts by famous architects who include Daniel Burnham, Louis Sullivan, Frank Lloyd Wright and Mies Van der Rohe. These architectural wonders demonstrated how gifted and unlimited men could be. However, in my extended tour of several days I saw another Chicago that was untouched by the creative and artistic hands of the master rebuilders. This Chicago was fraught with overcrowded tenement housing, illicit drug use, slumlords, unemployment, teen pregnancy and inadequate education. The startling contrast between the privileged and the under privileged resembled some places in the South. However, the difference was the squalor was vertical in the North and lateral in the South. It became clear to me that there were major inequities in city services and resources. Again, the majority of the underprivileged were black Americans who were still in search of the promised land.

I soon learned that many people who relocated to large industrial northern cities, such as St. Louis, Detroit, Chicago, and Gary, experienced inner emotional conflict. The conflict was centered on anguish and bewilderment for having left the South where community and extended family ties were important for the unfriendly ghettoes in the North. In many cases their hopes for a better future, were daunted by the continuing nightmare of social rejection and racial segregation. They found that black Americans experienced rejection in the North as they did in the South. Chicago, Detroit, Gary, and Saint Louis were often referred to as up south.

I resided on the south side of Chicago in a racially segregated neighborhood that had been abandoned by white families because of the fear of integration. My neighbors were predominantly college graduates and working professionals. While the city amenities and service were much improved over many black residential communities, there were still vestiges of blight that were ignored by city services.

a. Victory In Spite of Odds

After arriving in Chicago, I rapidly turned to securing employment for my new self-supporting status. I reported to the Chicago Board of Education to apply for teaching assignment. Once the written application was completed I was told to report to the medical unit for a medical examination. The examining doctor discovered that I had a heart murmur, which indicated a cardiac abnormality. He told me that I should consult a cardiac specialist who could diagnose my case more thoroughly. I was distraught and discouraged. After all, I had completed my college requirements to launch a career in teaching. I relocated from New Orleans for the purpose of teaching school only to come to a total roadblock with no idea of a resolution. I considered returning to New Orleans in defeat or taking my life in my hands and seeking a solution toward good health.

My uncle, who was a very resourceful businessman, owned a building that housed a nursery for children, a pharmacy, and a suite of offices occupied by an internal medical doctor by the name of William London. He discussed my case with Dr. London, who was doing a residency under Dr. Benjamin Kaplan, a cardiologist. Dr. Kaplan was interested in meeting me for observation and possible treatment. After my examination he contacted a friend of his, Dr. Laurence Rubenstein, who was a cardiac surgeon. The two doctors compared the results of their examination of me and concluded that I should have surgery for correction of a coarctation of the aorta. This condition caused hypertension in the upper extremities of my body and low pulsation in the lower extremities, thereby, producing a heart murmur. Hypertension was a constant sign of the illness, which could have resulted in a stroke early in my life. I had lived with this condition for 22 years with no outward sign that would have indicated danger. When I was 11 years old I was admitted to the hospital for a routine tonsillectomy and the doctors became frustrated with what appeared to be an erratic sound in my heart.

Because of the uncertainty of my condition I was discharged from the hospital without having my tonsils removed. I spent the next six years in the care of doctors and medical technicians studying my condition. Surgeons who wanted to perform surgery on me constantly approached me but my parents were not confident enough in medical technology at that time. I continued my life with normal activity until my encounter with the physician at the Chicago Board of Education in 1959. At the age of 22, I had come to the time of my own decision-making and I was advised that continuing my life with such complications could lead to a serious stroke or death. I have always had a strong faith and total reliance on God. After consultation with my parents, I submitted to having the surgery. After telling them of my strong faith in arriving at the decision, they supported my decision to have surgery.

I was admitted to Michael Reese Hospital on August 20, 1959, and began many tests and preparations for surgery. There seemed to be no end to the doctors, medical students, and medical technicians with great interest in my case. On August 26th, the eve of surgery, a young male medical intern who had a poor bedside manner visited me. He was not supportive nor was he encouraging. He told me that I had a 50% chance of not coming out of surgery successfully and that it was not a routine procedure especially having never been done before. This insensitive message left me quite depressed and uncertain as to whether I had made the right decision. I cried myself to sleep, only to be awakened by a team of medical personnel who readied me for the ordeal. Prior to surgery they allowed me to see my mother who had a look of total confidence on her face; her countenance was calming and somewhat serene. I began to feel that I was safe from all harm and I experienced a peace as never before. I was taken into the operating room, and the last words that I heard were the words of my mother saying, "Don't worry, Junior, everything will be alright." I remained convinced that my mother's strong faith allowed me to endure the medical ordeal with a positive attitude and total dependence on God. I saw the medical team, dressed in white, standing over me. I told them that they looked like angels. I awoke after surgery 12 hours later. The first face that I saw was the face of my mother whom I could faintly hear saying, "junior. They said that the surgery was successful, I told you it would be alright." After recuperation, I returned to the Chicago Board of Education in October. I reapplied for the teaching position and was hired.

After all I had been through, I knew that I had an obligation to give something to humanity that would enhance other lives, and serve as a witness as to what surrender to an unconditional faith can yield. The physical and educational development of our children of need was a call to me to go and serve. My lifelong thanks continue for the belief in miracles of my mother, my uncle and aunt, Drs. London, Kaplan, and Rubenstein whose skillful surgical hands corrected my malady.

b. The Children of Need

Being hired to teach in the Chicago school system was the first hurdle to overcome, finding a school where a vacancy existed and gaining acceptance was the second. Celeste Banks Taylor, a friend and college mate also from New Orleans, was teaching at the Nathaniel Pope Elementary School where there was a vacancy. She informed me that her principal was in need of a teacher. She assisted me in making arrangements to be interviewed by Mr. Charles LaForce, who subsequently hired me for the position. The job gave me a feeling of really giving something back after all that had been given me. The school was located in the Douglas Park section of the west side of Chicago and was named for a man who served in several political capacities, the last being a judge for the District of Illinois, from 1818 to 1850. The neighborhood was known for its inadequate housing and slum dwellings, illiteracy, dysfunctional families, and widespread poverty. I was assigned a fourth grade class where I taught the basic remedial subjects of reading, writing and arithmetic. These subjects were offered to students who were fraught with myriad social problems and had difficult time learning. The school system was geared to providing a basic curriculum for learning; but more specialized education was needed in the areas of building self esteem, the practice of good health habits, positive social relationships and good citizenship. The school was 90% black American. Most of the faculty was white and not in tune with the comprehensive needs of the students.

Many of them were not residents of the inner city, which was a complicated dynamic in itself. This contributed to a barrier in intimately understanding the crucial needs of children who lived in overcrowded conditions with meager resources. There was a constant struggle to understand the difference in race and culture and how to reach students who had a propensity to learn but not according to the conventional standards of education.

The principal was a white male of towering physical proportion, and was more of a keeper of the peace and order than an educator. In many instances, teachers and students feared suspensions or expulsions from the administration for minor infractions. Recognizing the true needs of the students, I joined a task force of some other teachers that was organized to assist the students in improving their grade point averages. Each teacher took one subject and worked with small groups to encourage more teacher attention and a better understanding of the subject matter as to how it related to their every day lives. This effort yielded an appreciable difference in the students learning ability. In my contributions to the task force effort I also taught music and performing arts to bring about a balance to the rigors of regular study. Non-traditional activities were often included in their course of study which their creative strengths demonstrated more promise. We would identify their comfort zone for learning and make it a joyful experience. The task force developed an approach to learning that helped the students build self-esteem, self-reliance and a can -do attitude.

Black American residential neighborhoods on the west side of Chicago were seen as trapped enclaves with no way out of deprivation unless you were a student with exceptional athletic or musical abilities. These disciplines could be a dead end if education had been neglected. The hope for the future for many black Americans who resided in the Douglas Park community was to invest in positive support of the youth as a community effort. Too often I witnessed the children from these desolate conditions succumb to welfare dependence, incarceration and sometimes death.

According to some sociologists, black American male youth are confronted with major social challenges that their white counterparts do not experience. They are more likely to be classified as mentally retarded with learning disabilities before being given an opportunity to prove themselves otherwise. They are more likely to be relegated to classes in general or vocational education than toward college preparatory courses. They have a greater school suspension rate than any other race or culture. This was especially true during my years as a student in the New Orleans public school system. Many black American males were victimized by negative attitudes from teachers, parents and administrative personnel, which only aid their failure. This social dynamic was demonstrated against black American males in Douglas Park in the late 1950s, still exist. Very little has been done in offering hope to the embattled black male.

The students that I taught at Pope Elementary were categorized as slow learners with no hope of socio-economic success. Because of the limited number of dedicated teachers who truly cared and sacrificed extra hours of instruction, a very small percentage of Pope's students succeeded in going to institutions of higher learning. It is a foregone conclusion that the mainstream population, which does not acknowledge their existence, thwarts the American dream for many black American youths. My experience at Pope Elementary revealed an unfeeling school system with political operatives and degrees of racism. It is vital to black American life that our youth are empowered, especially the black American male. They are entitled to thoughtful and instructive guidance toward achieving academic goals and challenges. This approach is not the responsibility of educator alone, but belongs in a comprehensive way to a caring community.

The Pope Elementary School experience was a true awakening of what lies in the future for those who are forgotten; they are counted as failures. This period of my life, as had the Montgomery bus boycott, caused me to focus my energies on helping those who found difficulty negotiating every day life situations. Recognizing the dilemma in the sociological and educational development of students, I was instrumental with other caring teachers in organizing homogeneous groups of students to improve their learning abilities. This approach to education specifically addressed itself to building self-esteem and self-confidence. I discovered that when students are placed in a caring and supportive environment their possibilities are unlimited.

c. Friends in the City

Teaching in an underprivileged school system proved to be a rewarding challenge for me. There were problems with dysfunctional families, the insensitive system to the black American. Many of the students had determination and family support, which yielded success in almost impossible situations. After five years of teaching, I to was anxious to rejoin the social movement and fight for civil rights in the school system, housing and employment. I became restless, as I looked for another vehicle to effect self empowerment. During the summer of 1964, my cousin, Sam Dennis, alerted me about an internship program. Sam was working for the Catholic Interracial Council in the field of race relations, and was privy to information about other race relation's efforts in the country. He told me about an internship opportunity with the Eleanor Roosevelt Memorial Foundation. The foundation was established in the 1960s to further the cause of human rights in areas where financial resources were not readily available. The National Association of Intergroup Relations Officials - NAIRO, managed the program. NAIRO was a group of people working within and outside of the federal government programs that intended to enhance racial and economic balance in American life. The emphasis of NAIRO was on education, employment, housing and fair treatment to all citizens. I applied for an internship and was accepted. I was given an opportunity to select an agency from a list of participating organizations, where I would perform one year of service. The arrangement was that NAIRO would contribute one half of the intern salary and the participating agency would contribute half. After reviewing the list of agencies I chose the American Friends Service Committee, AFSC. The Friends, as they were commonly referred to, is the social action component of the Religious Society of Friends, Quakers. The American Friends Service Committee is a Quaker organization, which includes people of various faiths and is committed to social justice, peace and humanitarian service. Its work is based on the belief in the worth of every person, and faith in the power of love to overcome violence and injustice. The Quakers have a long history of involvement whenever the rights of any people are abridged. They were prominently involved in the Underground Railroad, which was a vehicle to freedom for many black American slaves. They were further involved in the establishment of European refugee camps during World War II. I chose the Friends because of nonviolent commitment and dedication to ethical and moral matters. Their work enhances the lives of people who are usually exploited economically, politically, psychologically, and culturally. The AFSC was a natural place for me to get reengaged in social change, especially given my earlier experience in the nonviolent Civil Rights Movement in Montgomery.

I began my work at Friends in September of 1964 in the housing program office. I witnessed the inequitable housing system throughout the city of Chicago. The city was operating under a weak fair housing ordinance that guaranteed fair and equitable housing opportunities to all citizens, regardless of race, color, or creed. The words were printed on paper but never carried out in practice. There was a dual real estate system, one for whites and one for blacks. The system directed blacks to less desirable housing neighborhoods while reserving the more desirable housing for whites.

Blacks who worked in many all white areas of the city, and desired to live closer to their places of employment, were regularly discouraged by the real estate industry. Housing discrimination against blacks was common practice of the time and the real estate system ignored the claims of housing inequities.

Prior to my arrival for my internship, the housing Opportunities Program was involved in supporting state legislation that would advance the cause of equitable housing. As a stopgap measure, we initiated a program called Home Opportunities Made Equal, Incorporated, HOME, INC. This was a volunteer realty brokerage effort that brought willing black homebuyers together with willing white home sellers in nontraditional black neighborhoods. This initiative circumvented the established real estate system and was supported by many white people. The emergence of HOME, INC. became an issue for the Chicago real estate industry, because housing sales were being negotiated and sold outside of their system, thereby causing a loss of real estate fees. Local neighborhood fair housing committees facilitated the sales. They were comprised of volunteers who matched a willing white home seller with a willing black buyer. This program lasted for approximately four years before more made housing equity their everyday practice.

In 1965, I launched a housing testing program to check the adherence to the Chicago Housing Ordinance. The testing procedure was carried out by sending a volunteer white couple to a designated real estate office to request a certain kind of house in a specific traditional white neighborhood for a specific price. Usually the real estate agent's response would be that such a house was available for the requested price. Next we sent a black couple to the same real estate office to request the identical housing specifications. They were always turned away or directed to a more traditional black neighborhood. After many test cases were reviewed and determined to be blatant cases of discrimination, we filed them with the Chicago Human Relations Commission for equitable dispensation. After several complaints were denied we concluded that the commission was supportive of the discriminatory practices of the real estate industry. Herein were cases made for public direct action.

During the spring of 1965, Dr. Martin Luther King, Jr. and the Southern Christian Leadership Conference, SCLC, became concerned that the world perceived racial segregation in America as limited to the South with the North seeming to be a utopia for all races and cultures. The migration to the North in the early 1900s proved that bigoted racial practices were also a large part of the migration. It became clear that SCLC had no other choice but to select a northern city to heighten world awareness that racial discrimination is a fact of American life in the South and in the North.

The late William Moyer, with whom I worked, and I developed a working paper about the inequity of housing in Chicago, This paper was founded on the exorbitant number of housing test cases that were coordinated and processed under my guidance over a number of months. We thought that the racial issues in the city of Chicago would be of interest to the SCLC, and we shared the paper with Dr. King and his staff. SCLC did an analysis to determine whether Chicago was a good demonstration city to demonstrate the blatant presence of segregation in the North.

Chicago was made up of neighborhoods of cultures that were highly celebrated, and prevalent with racism. The European ethnic groups consisting of Irish, Italian, and Slovakian, and a limited population of Jewish people, resided in the immediate west and northwest neighborhoods. Hispanics took up residence at the north and southwestern fringes of the Chicago River, and black neighborhoods were clearly marked on the south and west sides of the city. Under Dr. King's leadership, Chicago was selected as the northern city that would be examined for evidence of discrimination. The SCLC could have easily chosen Detroit, Saint Louis or New York City and found similar conditions, but Chicago was chosen instead. It proved to be an excellent choice to make the point.

During the summer of 1965 the staff and volunteers from the SCLC began to arrive in Chicago to prepare for the northern campaign. The first contingent was a group of young black and white demonstrators fresh from the Selma, Alabama demonstrations. Some having come from the jails others being sought by southern authorities for disturbing the peace of the tranquil south, and attempting to vote. They came full of energy, somewhat rowdy, cocky but respectful. They came attired in what became known as "Movement Garb," Bibbed overalls blue denim shirts and work shoes. They were in Chicago, ready to repeat their civil disobedience activities as they had done in the South. They were in a festive mood, showing no signs of fear or shame. They were soldiers of Freedom singing the old Negro Spirituals, such as: *Aint gwa let nobody turn me 'roun, What side are you on, boy, Keep yo eyes on de prize, Oh, freedom, Freedom's comin an it wont be long, and We shall overcome.*

Many of the black Chicagoans were not happy to see their southern brothers and sisters dressed in farm attire, bibbed overalls, blue denim shirts, and work boots. After all, they had arrived at a status of respectability. They were embarrassed by the manner in which the SCLC staff dressed and behaved in ways that seemed uncouth. What was not taken into account were the constant threats by the law enforcement agencies that the SCLC staff lived under daily. There was constant pressure of living under the threat of jails, police brutality and death. Because of our experiences in demonstrations, and harsh treatment by authorities, we were different, and prepared to go the distance for freedom. We were trained in the art of nonviolence in the face of violence perpetrated against us. The excruciating long hours of non-violent workshops prepared us for the reaction from those who opposed our quest for freedom. We learned to smile when struck, pray when verbally attacked, and consistently practice the principles of Jesus Christ, and Mahatma Gandhi when under siege. We learned that the non-violent demonstrator channeled his/her normal aggression through periods of self-cleansing, fasting, and prayer.

Early in the summer the SCLC, Urban League, NAACP, Catholic Interracial Council, Coordinating Council of Community Organizations, Community Renewal Foundation, and the Chicago Council of Churches sponsored the Chicago Freedom Rally at Soldier Field where approximately 25,000 Chicagoans attended. The Honorable Mayor Richard J. Daley was one of the speakers, but was booed and heckled by a segment of the crowed until he stormed off the stage in anger, and was rushed off in an automobile. This was the beginning of the infamous contentious Chicago summer of 1966, where I was to play a definitive role as one of the major leaders of the Chicago Freedom Movement. After other speakers approached the podium and spoke, Martin Luther King's moment had arrived. He delivered the keynote address. His remarks centered on the tremendous wealth of America's third largest city, and the increasing numbers of black Americans who were among the nation's poorest of the poor. He spoke of the segregated housing dilemma and how blacks were relegated to substandard communities. The rally signaled a threshold to a transformation of racial relations in Chicago, and a warning for America of urban unrest in the days to come. In the winter of 1965 there were many SCLC neighborhood workshops on nonviolent demonstrations. These workshops taught us how to peacefully conduct ourselves when under physical attack. King required his followers to adhere to the philosophy of nonviolence in the following ways:

1. That they be courageous and offer non-resistance not through fear or cowardice or lack of weapons but through a conviction in rightness of their cause;
2. That they seek reconciliation and friendly understanding from their opponents rather than victory over them
3. That they direct their energy against the unjust situation and not against the people who perpetuate it;
4. That they be willing to accept suffering, pain, humiliation, jail and even death to prove the righteousness of their cause and also bear this degradation without retaliation;
5. That the nonviolent resisters cleanse themselves of hate and instead, show love and consideration for their opponents; and
6. That they believe that cause to be just and to have faith in the future and a peaceful and harmonious settlement of the dispute.

The workshops proved to be valuable instructions for future application of nonviolence in a violent climate. It was important to constantly encourage would-be demonstrators to be vigilant in their understanding of the cause for which we were involved. Basic teachings of the philosophy of Mahatma Gandhi served as a basic point of pride that black Americans could rely on in times of doubt and fear. Lerone Bennett cites an encouraging writing by Gandhi in 1929, which was, ironically, the year of King's birth, Gandhi wrote:

"Let not the twelve million Negroes be ashamed of the fact that they are the grandchildren of slaves. There is no dishonor in being slaves. There is dishonor in being slave owners. But let us not think of honor or dishonor in connection with the past. Let us realize that the future is with those who would be truthful, pure and loving. For as the old wise men have said, truth ever is, untruth never was. Love alone binds, and truth and love accrues only the truly humble. Perhaps it will be through the Negro that unadulterated messages of nonviolence will be delivered to the world."

In preparation for the oncoming nonviolent demonstrations, many community meetings were held to educate the community about the cause and eventual benefits. Church participation was solicited, community organizations were courted for participation and agreement on issues, the egos of clergy had to be stroked, many meetings with city officials, and a concerted agenda had to be established.

d. Nonviolent Engagement

In May of 1966, King requested that I assume the directorship of the South Side Action Center of the Chicago Freedom Movement. This was to be the base of operations for the movement over the summer months. The center's office was located in the basement of the Educational Building of the Friendship Baptist Church. Pastor Stroy Freeman and the membership of the church were gracious enough to permit SCLC to use the space. With the cooperation of the American Friends Service Committee, I was permitted to give my time, totally, to the Chicago Freedom Movement. I conducted an all-volunteer staff of nine people, and a host of part- time volunteers who took on ad hoc assignments. More specifically, the purpose of the center was to plan and execute community-wide mass meetings to reporting and update the community on the progress of the movement, solicit more participation, raise funds for administrative operations, and bail for jail, organize demonstrations, facilitate nonviolent workshops, and provide a forum for dialogue on current issues that adversely affected black Chicago citizens.

The summer of 1966 was a violent and dramatic campaign for addressing the inequitable dual housing market. The demonstrations were in the form of peaceful prayer marches into neighborhoods that were traditionally white. These marches were usually directed to a specific neighborhood or real estate office, because of their practice of discrimination. Here, we got the chance to put into practice all we learned in the nonviolent workshops. We were, predictably, met by angry mobs of white people who were relentless in their attempts to prevent any blacks from relocating into

I Shall Not Pass This Way Again

their neighborhoods. They spat on us, threw blunt and sharp missiles, and even pushed several automobiles of the demonstrator's automobile convoy into a nearby lagoon that was full of water.

The city police, who were assigned to keep law and order, stood by and did nothing to stop the disorderly behavior. They applied no law enforcement tactics as they witnessed many of our demonstrators suffering at the hands of the unruly crowd. The blood of many demonstrators left on the streets of Gage and Marquette Parks will always be an indelible mark signifying the price of freedom for a disavowed people. There were times when the police, who were on duty to keep order, seemed to be on the side of the hecklers. The demonstrators were being attacked and beaten badly by the hecklers and the police did nothing to prevent it. The violence became a concern for onlookers around the nation. This placed Chicago in a bad light. Mayor Daley issued orders to the chief of police to restrain the hecklers from more attacks on demonstrators. The police immediately reversed their tactics and began to heavily restrain the hecklers by beating them with truncheons and causing much blood shed. In the true spirit of nonviolence, King made a strong request to the mayor to cease the brutal retaliatory measures that were being administered to the hecklers by the police.

Hate was so very pronounced that many unseasoned demonstrators failed to return for continuous demonstrations, however, others heard of the violent treatment and felt compelled to become a part of history in the making. As a veteran of the civil rights movement, I was not ready for the counter demonstrations by white residents as was evidenced in Chicago. There were acts of practiced hateful reactions. I remember hearing the lyrics of a song that was sung by the throngs of white youth as we marched passed them. The song was set to the melody of the Oscar Meyer Weiner commercial jingle:

> *I wish I were an Alabama Trooper that is what I'd truly like to be. 'Cause, if I were an Alabama Trooper, then I could kill the niggers legally.*

I often thought if the hecklers decided to ignore the demonstrators, the movement would fall on its own weight. They could not resist a confrontation, and we needed them to attack, because their adverse behavior gave the movement momentum, and made the cause a just one. I became an integral entity in Chicago. I found that King depended on my contributions to plan and execute the demonstrations. I was an effective member of a team of passionate and committed people working under the guiding philosophy of Martin Luther King, Jr., Reverends Andrew Young, Jesse Jackson, C.T. Vivian, Ralph Abernathy, Alvin Pitcher, Bernard Lafayette, James Bevel, and many others. After a long week of preparation, demonstrations were held in different white neighborhoods each Sunday afternoon, and some evening events around real estate offices and resistant neighborhoods.

The demonstrations continued throughout the summer, even after an attempt on King's life in Marquette Park. A man was determined to take King's life with a knife but his bodyguards were able to prevent the attempt.

The city was in turmoil, and little or no progress was being made in our attempts to make breakthroughs toward equal housing opportunities. The fate of the Chicago Freedom Movement seemed doomed. There was no compromise from the white community or the city leaders. What appeared to be a complete breakdown of law and order became of interest around the world.

The summer's activities had reached such a stalemate that it became necessary for King to call a brief secession of the demonstrations and request a meeting with the mayor and his advisors. I was asked to join King and a host of Chicago Freedom Movement operatives as representatives of the Chicago Freedom Movement. The meeting was held at the rectory of Saint Joseph's Catholic Church for over nine hours. It was reported that the mayor had never attended a meeting about community concerns in the history of his mayoralty. After many accusations and disagreements across the meeting table, Andrew Young suggested to the mayor that if we didn't come to an amicable agreement about the issues that were being discussed, SCLC would not be responsible for adverse reaction from the black community. The mayor quickly responded to Young with the question, "Are you telling me that there will be violence in the city of Chicago?" Young put the statement to rest by stating that there are people in Chicago who do not adhere to King's nonviolent philosophy, and that we should be judicious and equitable in the results of the meeting.

In an effort to make progress, the mayor offered what he thought to be a remedy to the stalemate. He proposed that certain organizations from the movement and the city form a biracial committee to examine the charges of housing discrimination and other added infractions against black people and come up with a recommendation to resolve the issues. The mayor had one condition in his proposal, which was for King to call a permanent secession to the demonstrations. King and his contingents asked for a recess to ponder the proposal by the mayor.

We assembled in a small meeting room in the rectory and discussed the advantages and disadvantages of the proposal. The leaders of the more mainline organizations such as the Urban League, Chicago Council of Churches, Catholic Interracial Council, and the American Friends Service Committee encouraged King to accept the mayor's proposal. This position was totally unacceptable to those of us who had lived in the trenches of the movement, those who had gone to jail for their beliefs, and those of us who had spent endless hours testing the real estate system and finding it grossly discriminatory. We felt it unreasonable to fall for a ploy of turning the movement's demands over to those who traditionally devalued our grievances. I was very much involved with the faction that felt that the mayor was at a breaking point, and that if we threatened more demonstrations to come unless we had a favorable agreement, we would have made our point. We saw the mayor's proposal as a stalling tactic with no intention of an equitable agreement. King was persuaded to take the advice of the traditional leaders, which meant that the mayor had won again. The decision to stop the demonstrations and to accept the mayor's proposal was one of the darkest periods of my life. Our commitment to a just cause and the dream of victory over a recalcitrant racist city had completely become a nightmare by the opposition using the same familiar tactics, divide and conquer. Some of us knew quite well the type of persons who would be left to work out so-called solutions. We demonstrated against discrimination in Chicago, we taught in Chicago, and we derived no benefits from Chicago. The civil rights movement was undermined, and as a result, the gains we suffered for never materialized. We were disappointed in political and selfish motives of key players on both sides. They had much to gain by the status quo.

Before the summit meeting with the mayor, a demonstration was planned to take place in Cicero, Illinois. Cicero was a working class community of white ethnics who resisted any attempt at housing integration in their community. The plans were developed in my office with great anticipation to march through the neighborhood. The march route was conceptualized and mapped by a young white civil rights activist from the U.S. Air Force Academy. King officially called off the march, because he was true to his word in his agreement with the mayor. However, there were others who were vehement about abandoning the Cicero march, and were in opposition to the agreement. Robert "Bob" Lucas led a small group through Cicero on his own accord without incident. Most observers credit King and SCLC with braving Cicero but SCLC never demonstrated in that neighborhood. It was a brave man and a few devoted followers on a lonely Sunday afternoon.

For all practical purposes, the Chicago freedom movement had come to an end. King made his last speaking appearance in Chicago on March 25, 1967. He spoke of his passion for peace in Vietnam. I shut down the South Side Action Center but not without acknowledging that the summer of 1966 was an emphatic lesson for all involved. The world came to know that racial hatred and segregation is not relegated to the South alone. The North vigorously held unrelenting demagogues of ill will. The Chicago campaign was a perplexing experience, while we did not force the real estate system to do business in an equitable manner, we did teach the world that America is suffering with a social cancer called racism. Our labor was not in vain. However, along with many others, I was left dejected, disappointed, and defeated, because of the movement's acquiescence to the mayor's meaningless proposal to call cessation to the effective demonstrations for a status quo committee to work on racial issues. At the writing of this book, Chicago continues to struggle with fair housing. The question of where do I go from here, became paramount in my continuous search for justice and freedom.

CHAPTER V

NEW HORIZONS

The answer of where to go next came quickly for me in November of 1967, when I accepted a position with the National Urban Coalition in Washington, D.C. The Urban Coalition was corporate America's response to urban unrest across the country. Detroit, Chicago, St. Louis, and south central Los Angeles were all experiencing social violent upheavals that included burning, destruction of property, and civil disobedience.

I was hired to serve as the associate director of the northeast region of the United States. My assignment was to organize urban multicultural forums for dialogue on issues of inequitable opportunities for minority persons. While I was working for the Urban Coalition, King was in Atlanta making plans for the Poor Peoples Campaign. The campaign was to be staged in Washington, D.C. during the summer of 1968. However, because of the growing discontent among the sanitation workers in Memphis, King was asked to go and offer some assistance to them in their labor dispute with the city. Two black workers were crushed to death when a mechanical malfunction was triggered. In addition to the deaths 22 black sewer workers were relieved of their duties and sent home without salary. Their white supervisors were allowed to continue working for pay. This act of inequity resulted in a strike involving over 1,000 black workers. They had reached an intolerable level of dissatisfaction. Good- willed white and black civic associations offered positive resolutions to Mayor Henry Loeb, who relentlessly opposed anything that involved the workers union. As a result of the mayor's recalcitrance, the momentum grew.

King interrupted his schedule of planning the Poor People's Campaign to accept a speaking engagement at a rally in Memphis on March 18. He gave his word that he would lead a large march that was planned to take place on March 28. This march did not take place, because many of the participants failed to carry out the spirit of nonviolence. Violence distressed King so much that he and fellow SCLC workers devised a plan of nonviolence with the dissenting factions of demonstrators. On April 4, Reverends James Lawson and Andrew Young worked out an arrangement with a judge to permit the march to take place on April 5. With the date set, Young relayed the news to King as they were preparing to have dinner before the mass meeting. King stepped outside of his room at the Lorraine Hotel and spoke to Ben Branch, the saxophonist who was to provide the music for the meeting, He asked him to play the Thomas Dorsey song, "Precious Lord." While he was talking, it was reported that the crack of gunfire snuffed out King's life. I was attending a meeting at the Poor Peoples campaign headquarters at Fourteenth and U Streets Northwest in Washington, D.C. The headquarters was located in a vacant bank building, where many workers had gathered for planning purposes. The noise level was so high we barely heard the telephone ring. I interrupted my meeting and answered the call, which had a sound like a long distance call. It was someone from Memphis informing us that King had been shot. His fate was not yet known. A second call followed about 10 minutes later to inform us that he was dead.

When the word about King's death was known on the streets of Washington, the streets became a violent battleground. I saw young black men stopping automobiles that were occupied by white persons and attacking them with a vengeance. There was a craze in the atmosphere that was completely out of hand. Men and women were audibly sobbing in the streets, and it was if hope for freedom had vanished out of sight. The police were at a loss in trying to control the situation. This riotous behavior continued for several days and nights until the D.C. National Guard was dispatched to restore order. The sentiments over the death of King were felt all over the country, with similar violent reactions.

On April 5, under the direction of U.S. Attorney Ramsey Clark, the FBI began an international manhunt for the assassin of King. While the search was underway, the sanitation worker's grievances were still unsettled. President Lyndon Johnson instructed Under Secretary of Labor James Reynolds to take charge of mediation to settle the sanitation strike. On Tuesday, April 9, still shaken by King's death and the violent aftermaths in some of our major cities. I departed Washington with John Gardner, and other members of the National Urban Coalition. We were headed to Atlanta to attend King's funeral at Moorehouse College. During the funeral, Morehouse became a sanctuary for mourners and the grief stricken. The sight of his widow and children experiencing their loss was heart rending, as the entertainer, Harry Belafonte and his wife Julie, comforted them. The SCLC staff was terribly encumbered with grief as they mourned the loss of the spirit of the movement.

After the funeral, at the call of Fauntroy, a small group of us gathered in Washington to finalize the plans for the Poor Peoples Campaign. Young, Fauntroy and Abernathy made a visit to John Gardner at the National Urban Coalition Offices and requested my help as a loaned staff person to the Poor People's Campaign. Gardner agreed and I was off to continue my direct action work with SCLC. The first order of business was to make arrangements with the U.S. National Park Services to provide the SCLC with a land use permit to occupy a portion of the land on the Federal Mall. The land that was requested was between the U.S. Capitol Building and the Lincoln Memorial. We gave the name "Resurrection City" to the site, which was developed by volunteer architects, carpenters, and electrical contractors. I was designated by Fauntroy and a delegation of organizers to serve in the capacity of Resurrection City Manager. Early in June of 1968, the non-working poor began to stream into Washington to take part in making King's dream a reality by the manifestation of the poor people of America before the eyes of the U.S. Congress. black, white, Native Americans, and Hispanics all came to participate in a drama highlighting human poverty in America. I coordinated the erecting of the shanties where the demonstrators would reside, warehoused the food donations, made assignments of living quarters, arranged day care for the children of the demonstrators and organized groups of demonstrators who went to the U.S. Capitol, House, and Senate Office Buildings daily.

My position as city manager of Resurrection City was a complex experience because it was fraught with many of the problems that small cities experience. We struggled with a mass of people who were in dire need of multiple social support services that were not being met. I was regularly confronted with making on-the-spot decisions about the provision of limited resources of food, medical services, child care, school classes, recreational activities for children and the issues of criminal infractions. The Washington D.C. city government, under the leadership of Mayor Walter E. Washington, was gracious in providing many of the needed social services. The staged campaign lasted almost three months, but with limited success. We did not realize our original goal for Congress to pass meaningful legislation to alleviate the problems of the poor partly because of the absence of the presence of King. The Congress did act on some limited legislation, which provided some food to needy families in poor counties of America, and the senate approved a bill to underwrite the development of low-income housing. While the end result of the Poor People's Campaign was far from what King had envisioned, the point was made that there are, indeed, a diverse population of persons who exist below the scale of poverty in the flourishing American economy, and the Congress was made aware of their existence.

I take great delight in taking an emphatic role in the plight of the poor and disenfranchised and dramatizing their grievances before America's legislators. My involvement in this segment of the civil rights movement of 1968 gave rise to my pilgrimage in fulfilling the words of Jesus:

> *...You must love the Lord your God with all your heart, and with all your soul, and with all your strength, and with all your mind, and you must love your neighbor just as much as you love yourself.*

For me to have been responsible for the daily order and organization of Resurrection City was an exercise of the will to bring about wholeness, freedom and equality to people who were left out of the American system.

The time arrived when I realized that, I needed to pause long enough to focus on my personal fulfillment. When I left Chicago for Washington, I was romantically involved with a woman who later turned out to be an undisputed blessing from God. When I was a teenager I often prayed that I would be blessed one day with a devoted Christian woman. One who would be faithful and a good mother to our children. God heard my prayers and answered me with my marriage to Louise Kathryn Johnston on July 12, 1968. Walter Fauntroy served as our wedding officiant. Louise and I met at the American Friends Service Committee when we worked on the same staff. We were opposites by nature. She was shy, and demure always retreating to the shadows. I played life's stage with glee looking for the next curtain call. Louise had a young two-year-old son, Stephen Todd Jehnsen, from a previous short-lived marriage. In August of the same year, Louise and Stephen joined me in Washington to begin our lives together. On August 19, 1969, our first child was born, and we named her Angela Louise. On February 25, 1972, we were blessed with our second child, Gregory Elbert. Gregory inherited his mother's nature that is until he decides to be a comedian. Stephen, Angela, and Gregory grew up together intertwined with a bond of love for each other that serves as a model for what God means by unconditional love. Our family is a mirror of Louise's and my respective families, love and togetherness. We have not been disappointed by our children, and live with the hope that we have not disappointed them. Stephen currently lives in Florida, and working in his business of painting and aquarium building, Angela is a child psychologist in Richmond, Virginia and Gregory is a middle school history teacher in Alexandria, Virginia.

CHAPTER VI

URBAN RENEWAL

At the close of Resurrection City, I returned to the National Urban Coalition to continue my national assignment. I worked for two more years organizing local coalitions throughout the U. S. Like the rest of the country, Washington, D.C. was beginning rebuilding programs in the wake of the burnings. Mayor Washington designated five city neighborhoods as the areas that would qualify for the Housing and Urban Development Department's, sponsored Urban Renewal Program. The areas that qualified were called Neighborhood Development Program Areas- NDP. One of the positive aspects of the program was HUD's insistence on community participation in the rebuilding effort. The community participated in organized Project Area Committees made up of the citizens who were being affected by the program.

The Washington, D.C. renewal effort was conducted by the D.C. Redevelopment Land Agency— RLA—, quasi-federal agency, charged with the responsibility of urban renewal land development for Washington. In 1969, the RLA Board of Directors hired Melvin A. Mister, a young urban activist, to serve as the executive director of the agency. Mel, as he was called by close acquaintances, and I had been friends before his celebrated hiring. We met when he worked for the U.S. Conference of Mayors during a period of time when mayors from around the nation needed an organizational presence in Washington. Mel was intimately involved in urban matters, and brought excellent administrative skills to the job, underscored by his social passion for civil rights. He was asked to participate in changing the faces of some significant neighborhoods that had been greatly destroyed by the fires of rebellion and urban unrest. As I was winding down my tour at the Urban Coalition, Mel and I spent a good deal of time discussing the possibility of my joining him in the rebuilding effort. We talked over lunch for many months about using my experience and skills in building a coalition between RLA and the affected communities. Mel was the best man for the task of directing the urban renewal effort. He demonstrated a caring spirit for the underprivileged, and a strong will for doing the right thing. He inherited a well-equipped staff that was engaged in the disciplines of planning, engineering, mapping, legal matters, appraising properties, real estate management, property leasing, and HUD relations.

With the exception of the downtown commercial district of Washington, there was a dire need to understand how to relate and affect underprivileged neighborhoods especially in the participation process. Without taking no for an answer, Mel persisted. I acquiesced and accepted the challenge of working with the affected neighborhoods. I began working for RLA in September of 1970, as the senior projects director for Redevelopment and Community Relations. My responsibility was to coordinate and oversee involvement of affected citizens in the total renewal process. I began by hiring suitable and sensitive project directors for two rather volatile neighborhoods, Fourteenth Street and H Street. I hired a third project director for the Shaw School Urban Renewal Area, which provided a capability for beginning the process of fulfilling the HUD requirement of forming Neighborhood Project Area Committees, (PAC). These were committees of people from affected neighborhoods, charged with representing the will of the residents in the renewal process.

Each project had a different faction of citizens to serve. Fourteenth Street housed a large percent of renters who were young, vocal and rebellious while Shaw and H Street were more stable with home ownership and older residents. I organized the staff to concentrate on overseeing the projects with a guarantee of fairness and equity. Up until this period, Urban Renewal had a reputation of urban removal of black people, and having no regard for community. Fourteenth Street- Cardoza- was a major burned out commercial strip surrounded by dilapidated apartment buildings and deteriorated walkups. Crime, drugs, violence, mental illness, and dysfunctional family life were prevalent. Much of the devastation throughout the neighborhood was due to the lack of economic means. I was not only confronted with deteriorating housing structures but hopeless and distressed people.

Prior to my arrival at RLA I was briefed about the social dynamics of the Fourteenth Street Urban Renewal area. The community that had it's own rhythm and agenda for doing business with RLA. Many of the residents were young, with records of incarceration; others were vocal and fresh from the 1960s direct action civil rights movement. Unlike the other renewal areas that depended on social and governmental programs for survival, the community leaders were two black activists who were quite knowledgeable and aware of government rules and regulations that governed the urban renewal process, especially where law mandated community involvement.

The two community activists who were at the forefront of the rebuilding process were Richard Jones, director of the Concerned Citizens of Central Cardoza, CCCC and Leroy Hubbard, director of Concerned Residents of Upper Cardoza, CRUC. During my initial orientation, I visited Jones and Hubbard to introduce myself as the liaison between the community and government. I met them in their respective offices one-on-one.

Jones appeared intimidating and angry. He was approximately 5 feet and 5 inches tall and the scowl on his face signaled his disgust with the RLA's policies and plans for the future rebuilding effort. His primary concern was the exclusion of the community over what was to be built in the area. Prior to my arrival, an RLA project director Robert Leland was the staff person in charge of the direction that the Fourteenth Street project would take. Leland was an unrelenting man with definitive ideas about planning that almost ignored the will of the residents. Jones was furious with Leland and clashed with him each time they met. Most words that Jones used were profane, to accentuate his anger and displeasure over government officials assuming to know what was good for the community. Leland's white skin did not help the situation during this time of racial distrust.

Hubbard, on the other hand, was mild mannered and cooperative. He always looked for a common ground for meaningful dialogue and agreement. His manner of behavior as opposed to Jones is not in any way to describe Hubbard as a push over, because he was not when he did not agree, but he was more reasonable to deal with than Jones. Jones was guided by his full knowledge of HUD regulations, and his passion for assisting the people he represented. These men in their community organization leadership roles were quite mindful of who and what they represented. The average resident in the neighborhood was not very knowledgeable or vocal about the sophisticated urban renewal plans, and was not encouraged to know by those who preceded my tenure.

I arrived on the scene to employ my skills of community organizing and to bring integrity and respectful communication with a community of disheartened, disrespected, and disallowed people who felt that they did not count for much in the process. My primary action was to make an assessment of the impediments that prevented the process from moving forward. I met with Mel a month after my arrival to brief him on my assessment, and to seek his support and guidance. After I explained the impasse that the city had encountered with Leland and Jones, and that we needed a more respectful and positive communication level to be employed by representatives of the RLA, we agreed that Leland had outlived his usefulness in the project, and that he should be reassigned to other meaningful work outside of the Fourteenth Street Urban Renewal area. With Mel in agreement, I met again with Jones and Hubbard to express the change in personnel, which they agreed would be a good start toward progress.

It became necessary for me to hire an assistant to me who shared my interest and passion for bringing hope to the Fourteenth Street project. I hired Wilford"Wil" Jackson, who was a perfect fit for the perils that I faced on a daily basis, and was a natural in people relations. Before hiring a permanent project director, I requested that Wil assist me in the coordination of the Fourteenth Street project area, He did an impressive job with very little preparation. There was never a project site office as there were in the other projects where residents could visit to feel a part of the anticipated changes in their neighborhood. They needed a site office where they could informally stop in to discuss their feelings about the rebuilding plans that concerned them. Previously, meetings were held in the RLA's downtown offices, which appeared intimidating. I took the opportunity to make some basic changes in the community process that gave the people an integral part of their rebuilding effort.

Wil and I began to do walking tours of the project area in search of a location to establish a project field office. We found a burned-out furniture store that was boarded up on Fourteenth Street, which happened to be in the same block that Richard Jones' organization was located. The store was situated on the crest of the incline to upper Fourteenth Street, which gave high visibility to the urban renewal effort in the area. Within a month, we had the building rehabilitated and retrofitted for the community site office with a large red, white and green RLA sign that extended over the sidewalk. This symbol that signified that we had taken residence in an effort to do respectful business in the community.

The next step was to hire and assign full time staff to be available to the community. Wil's help was invaluable, as he was already in place as the coordinator of the Fourteenth Street project; however, his help was needed in other areas assuring community participation. HUD mandated in the dispensation of Urban Renewal Funds that project areas must have involved affected community personnel in the total process of rebuilding, and the manner in which it was prescribed was the community formation of Project Area Committees.

I met with Richard Jones and Leroy Hubbard, and several other Fourteenth Street area community representatives, to discuss the formation of a Fourteenth Street project area committee. After much discussion and disagreement about whether any one of the existing community organizations could be recognized as the representative organization, the RLA position was clear that no existing community organization represented an inclusive body of the community, therefore, a new organization had to be formed. After a series of community meetings, we came to a satisfying arrangement of an agreeable structure of the PAC. The organization was formed and entered into an agreement with the RLA. They were given the appropriate funding and the authority to hire planners, architects and community organizers to begin the legitimate process of planning and rebuilding.

This experience was not without major disagreements about replacement housing, commercial service centers, open space, rehabilitated housing and the age-old debate about who *really* speaks for the community," pork barrel" politicians or the affected people. There were times when those who wrongly professed to speak for the legitimate residents misled the RLA. By this time I had developed a trusting relationship with Richard Jones and Leroy Hubbard, and it was their uncompromising integrity that I came to trust. I knew that they represented the will of the people. We were now ready to move ahead.

TRANSFORMATION FROM OLD TO NEW

The time had come for full attention to be given to all of our urban renewal projects, with a timetable for completion. The Downtown Project was in good hands with Project Directors Michael Brimmer; H Street, N.E; Daniel Bankett; Shaw School; James Woolfork; Northwest #1, Harold Scott; and Southwest, Saul Finn. Fourteenth Street was still without a permanent Director until 1972 I hired Lacy Carroll Streeter, whom I had come to know from his days in the late 1960s at The Urban Institute in Washington, D.C. The Urban Institute is a nonprofit, nonpartisan organization dedicated to examining national economic, social and governance issues. I needed someone with an analytical mind and because of Lacy's work with the Urban Institute he was a good fit for the job. The Fourteenth Street project had reached the phase of development and building. I negotiated with Lacy to fill the project director vacancy. Prior to coming to an agreement with Lacy, Mayor Washington dispatched me to coordinate the razing of buildings in the Fourteenth Street project area, where new buildings were to be built. This job took about eight months. While the razing was underway, I hired Lacy to take the project into the development phase. He spent several months reviewing the project, and getting acquainted with the system of players in the community and government. We had now come to the point of transformation of the old to the new, which was to be handled in a politically sensitive, yet calculated manner. Lacy was to guide the project on top of the careful foundation that survived anger and distrust. Under my direction, Lacy approached his work with integrity and care of the civil rights worker that he was in the mid -1960s in Greensboro, North Carolina. The project was besieged with would- be housing developers looking for opportunities to leave their imprint in an area that was soaring out of the ashes of the summer of 1968. Despite the difficulties of arriving at an agreement with community, the high rising high cost of development, which had a debilitating affect on affordable rents and the debate on open land space, we realized 200 units of new affordable housing by 1974.

When my staff and I began our tenures with the RLA, we were novices in an all- white world of steel, concrete, and people planning but we went with the common sense that there is no mystery to treating humanity with dignity and respect, and having no respect for greed. We came with experience in human relations and that became the most important aspect of the urban renewal venture. To be believed and respected, especially by those who have been left out of the plans that affect their existence, is rewarding in many ways. Maintaining the delicate balance between the government and the community to be served requires a special sensitivity to humanity. So many times we witnessed the need for government to protect the community from pork-barreling politicians, who loved greed more than humanity.

When I tour the Urban Renewal areas of Washington, D.C., I feel immense pride about what it has become I tried to do what was right and set a table of brotherhood and sisterhood for all who were involved in the community transformation process. I am the richer, because of the many sleepless nights and endless meetings in the name of pride and dignity.

CHAPTER VII

THE BARRY YEARS

In 1978 Marion Barry became the second elected mayor of Washington, D.C. Because of his radical demeanor, his critics predicted that he did not have a chance. He ran third going into the primary elections on a platform of inclusion and progressive reform, overshadowing former Mayor Walter E. Washington and City council Chairman Sterling Tucker. This victory signaled Barry's tenacious nature and his willingness to go the distance to beat the odds.

Barry had an arrogant facade and a street manner that ingratiated him with those of the city who were excluded from the mainstream. He was a paradox in nature when you came to know him. When people dismissed him as a street ruffian, he would always rise to the occasion of refuting their assertions by brilliantly outflanking them with sound, intelligent judgment. He was a true study of sociology and politics; therefore, I viewed him as a sociopolitical phenomenon with a positive sense of victory. He had a deep passion for organizing people for particular tasks and choosing the right talents for the right jobs. He insisted on loyalty and good judgment, because he asked no less of himself. There are interesting parallels in our lives, that endeared me to his basic nature which is alien too much of his demonstrated social behavior. We share the year 1936 and the state of Mississippi as the year and location of our births. We, both, picked cotton in white- owned fields of Mississippi. He migrated from Mississippi to Memphis, Tennessee, and I migrated from Mississippi to New Orleans, Louisiana. He became active in the civil rights movement in college during the late 1950s, and into the turbulent 1960s, I too was active in the movement during the same period of time. Barry was in Tennessee and I was in Alabama. While on our separate but similar paths, we found each other in the nation's capitol, Washington, D.C. He arrived in 1964 and I arrived in 1967.

Prior to meeting Barry, I had heard about him from James Bevel and Bernard Lafayette, who were both involved in the SNCC field operations with Barry in Nashville. I finally met Barry in Washington when he was directing a neighborhood organization called Pride, Incorporated. Our meeting was by chance when I was doing community organization work for the National Urban Coalition. The second encounter with him was during the organizational efforts of the Poor People's Campaign. While serving as city manager of Resurrection City, it was Marion Barry who arranged for his workmen from Pride, Incorporated, to remove the garbage and refuse from the site in an arrangement between SCLC and Pride. Ten years later Marion Barry became my boss in his elected role as mayor of Washington, D C. He inherited a sluggish bureaucracy that was in need of reforms. By all accounts Barry was the lightening rod that was needed in Washington and he was the man for the job. He instituted a balanced financial accounting system, opened city government to the people, and operated an efficient city that served the citizens. His first term was the best and he gained the respect of the people. I worked in a very demanding position in the Barry Administration. I directed the real estate efforts for the city, which included leasing responsibilities, administrative space utilization, buildings management, and family and business resources. Because of my responsibilities, I had reasonable access to the mayor, and I found him to be a visionary with a definitive creative direction in making life better, especially, for those who were traditionally left outside of the system.

Unfortunately, the ensuing years were not as kind to Barry as his first term, it was alleged that he fell prey to alcohol and illicit drugs. Many people felt the need to provide him with as much help as possible. There were times that he and I had prayers together to allow him to feel the presence of love and caring. During this time, I chaired a monthly Christian Fellowship Luncheon Group that met at a beautiful mansion called "Cedars." It was located in Arlington, Virginia on a grassy knoll surrounded by cedar trees. This was a wonderful setting to be alone with your thoughts or to meditate, or to be with well- wishing friends. Barry often joined us for prayer and spiritual sustenance. These were times when his critics were vehemently active and he needed the nurture and care of friends in fellowship. I was invited to serve as the luncheon host by the late Herbert Barksdale, who was the sponsor of the event.

These were also turbulent times for many who were identified as being in the Barry Camp. While serving in my capacity as director of real estate, I was wrongly implicated in a matter in which I was eventually exonerated. This was a case of a suit against the District of Columbia Government for entering into a lease agreement, allegedly, with no authority to honor it. My department head affixed his signature to the lease, which was found to be null and void, rendering it ineffective. Because of my position, Thomas Downs, the City Manager, falsely implicated me. After a long investigation of facts, I was exonerated and found to be uninvolved. We later found that the mayor's political critics were at work to destroy him and all others around him. Eventually the case was amicably settled, after I spent four days before 14 lawyers as a creditable witness. The mayor completely supported my good reputation, and I shall remain ever grateful to him for this.

My work in the District of Columbia government was a true learning experience and one that has taught me the dark side of politics, while also providing times of gratification when a citizen would say to me, "thank you for making my life a little better." I gave my very best in the service of my several jobs, and seeing them as a constant ministry in doing well for humanity.

Barry had a good heart for the troubled and downhearted, even when a difficult decision had to be made that would protect or defend his honor. There were times when had to take adverse actions against someone who was contrary to the good of the city, in doing so, he would agonize over the ultimate outcome. A high-ranking city employee, and a friend of his became insubordinate and uncooperative over a city issue, and the mayor was left with no other choice but to separate him from his position by firing him. When the time came for the personnel papers to be signed, he lingered and anguished over the matter for an extraordinary length of time before he could bring himself to sign the document. I was with him at the time, and observed the inner pain he went through to act responsibly on this issue.

During my tenure with Barry I observed multiple personalities which indicated that he could have conceivably been clinically diagnosed as having multiple personality disorder. On one hand he was the consummate caring politician, and on the other he was a man who was determined to adversely alter his health and dilute his leadership effectiveness in his, alleged, participation in the illicit drug culture. In addition to these two distinct personalities, he could be observed as moody, and often withdrawn. While history will probably record his negative personal life, there is truly another man inside of Barry who will also be remembered as a visionary leader for the downtrodden, the disavowed and the disallowed…the least of our brothers and sisters. As the righteous are defined and judged by a higher authority, there shall come a day when Mayor Marion Barry, Jr. will be fully recognized for the good he did for humanity. The imperfections in his life will be fully forgiven as those who care and those who count recognize him. He, too, shall not pass this way again but his mark will be sorely left in the annals of history. Our paths intersected at a propitious time of the recognition of children of former Mississippi slaves who defied the odds in spite of the social obstacles. We have come a long way but we have many miles to go before we will have the full realization of freedom.

CHAPTER VIII

CALLED, COMPELLED AND CONVICTED

⇥≡⇤

P ast experiences in life can serve as the foundation on which the future rests. When one arrives at intersecting points of decision-making where choices are to be made about the rest of life's journey, it becomes necessary to explore the inner recesses of the soul for the answer.

In 1975 I took stock of the past 39 years of my life by taking an introspective view of who I was, and based on where I had been, and where I was going. My life up to this point had been an integration of good and not- so- good. It is difficult to live in a world that is fraught with evil and not be touched by the temptations, thereof. My past was a secret contradiction that allowed me to celebrate the dark and the light side of life at the same time. There comes a time when the inner spirit of man is at odds with outer behavior, which necessitates life adjustments.

While I was at a transforming point in my life, my family and I relocated to Alexandria, Virginia. In this quieter environment I found myself in an atmosphere of deep introspection. I found this community still imbedded and celebrating ante-bellum history in its preservation of 18th century architecture and the ghost of George Washington. Living in Alexandria provided me much time for reflection and introspection. After searching for inner peace and a closer relationship with God, I felt more and more that my true calling was to be a spiritual leader among those who yearned for a closer relationship with God. I had always been a believer in the sovereignty of God in making His will manifest in whomever He desired. I found myself in a struggle between responding to the urge to be a preacher and continuing my life as a government bureaucrat. This was during the time I worked for the RLA as the senior project director for Urban Renewal. I was responsible for a staff of 58 people and among them were nine ordained religious ministers who were responsible for responding to the affected churches in the project areas. One day I approached Fred X. Porter who was the pastor of Antioch Baptist Church, located in northeast Washington, D.C. I asked Porter to advise me as to how one becomes a minister, and his response was to find a church and join it. I was between churches and in search of a church home. I explained my struggle to him and he provided me with wise and sound counsel. I joined Antioch in 1974 and began preliminary training under Porter. As time passed, I prepared myself to be licensed by Antioch as a preacher. For two years, I practiced ministry under the auspices of the Antioch Congregation. The license provided me the opportunity to work as an apprentice under the pastor.

Antioch Baptist Church was approximately 35 miles from my residence in Alexandria, and the distance became a problem, especially since many Baptist churches surrounded me in my neighborhood. I left Antioch in 1976 and became a member of Alfred Street Baptist Church, located in Alexandria. In my constant pursuit of the gospel ministry, Alfred Street allowed me to transfer my license to that congregation. Alfred Street is an impressive church that is made up of people of education and economic means, as well as those who were not so fortunate. I saw Pastor Peterson as a progressive leader with influence in the Alexandria Community and the world. He has been able to assemble a congregation of resourceful persons who represent many facets of community life. The church was compartmentalized into multiple serving ministries that were coordinated by the ministerial staff and spiritually supported by assigned deacons. At the beginning of my Alfred Street responsibilities I joined Pastor Peterson as an assistant to the pastor in providing spiritual leadership to the congregation. This was a period of learning and serving. Because of my musical background, I was immediately assigned coordinator of the Music Department of seven choirs and instruments. The musicians were professionally trained and accomplished, each with the ability to perform solo concerts. I also served in other capacities, such as, worship leader, Bible study instructor, preacher, and counselor. During the spring of 1984, I began studying for ordination, which compounded my studying habits while continuing seminary studies. Preparing for ordination was a family enterprise. My wife and our children participated in helping me to prepare for the ordination council. They were as diligent and anxious as I was. My daughter, Angela, kept the 3x5 study note cards in her possession at all times to spot test me at any given moment. Eventually I was ordained at Alfred Street on December 1, 1984.

In 1986, I entered the Howard University School of Divinity for full seminary training toward a Master of Divinity Degree. Seminary was a place to learn how to use proven and tested resources to advance the story of Jesus Christ. I was asked to organize a chapel choir of seminarians to provide music in song at all chapel services. The choir became a necessary part of the seminary worship experience and added a new dimension to the student and faculty congregation. In this role as chapel choir director I was able to bring new meaning to seminary life in the medium of prayer through song. The advent of the choir came out of a request, made by Dr. H. Donald Kortwright Davis, Professor of Systematic Theology. Dr. Davis had the responsibility for planning chapel services, and was in need of some new ideas. I was attending his class one evening and he made the request to the class for someone to take on the responsibility of organizing a chapel choir. The class mused at the idea until someone said that I had majored in music and the job should be mine. I attempted to dodge the issue, however, Dr. Davis, with his native Caribbean persuasiveness, insisted that I assume the task, and I accepted it.

Howard School of Divinity was considered the black seminary experience, and although it was non-denominational, students playfully referred to each other as Bishop, Doctor, or Prelate. It was a comedic way of getting through the course work in an upbeat manner. During my study at Howard, Alfred Street served as a great laboratory for honing my ministerial skills and learning the practical aspects of being a pastor. As I grew, I began taking on more pastoral responsibilities, such as baptizing, leading Bible study, officiating the sacrament of communion, performing marriages, pastoral counseling, and home and hospital visits. These duties provided me with a true sense of Christian ministry and pastoral administration. The study at Howard prepared me to undergo deeper experiences in church and community leadership. My theological education grew because of professors such as Dean Lawrence Jones, Assistant Dean; Clarence Newsome, professor of New Testament Cain Hope Felder; professor of Old Testament, Gene Rice; and many others who dedicated part of their fields of endeavor toward expanding my theological sojourn.

Howard provided me with a solid ground for understanding the black Church experience and the traditional religious and social power of the black pulpit. Prior to my ministerial practice and studies at Howard, my impetus to enter the field of ministry was guided by men like Gardner C. Taylor, pastor emeritus, Concord Baptist Church, Brooklyn, New York; Nicholas Hood, former pastor of Central Congregational Church, New Orleans, Louisiana; Martin Luther King, Jr., late pastor of the Historical Dexter Avenue Baptist Church, Montgomery, Alabama; and Samuel DeWitt Proctor, pastor emeritus, Abyssinian Baptist Church, Harlem, New York. These were men of great vision for the future of America and the prominent place of Black people in it. With the realization of this vision, my life's course was fashioned and molded.

I was graduated from Howard in 1989, having earned the Master of Divinity Degree. In 1992 I enrolled at Wesley Theological Seminary in Washington, D.C. to begin work toward the Doctor of Ministry degree. The Wesley experience was quite different than Howard. The atmosphere was more formal with a deeply regarded observance for the Methodist principles on which it was founded. The classes were structured as seminars where each seminarian brought his or her life experiences to bear. This cross-fertilization of minds gave rise to a broader participatory learning process.

In an attempt to prepare myself for a more intense leadership role in the lives of people who were disavowed, disillusioned, and without a role in planning their destiny, I chose the path of concentrating on "servant hood." I selected a course of study that would help me give back to community all and more than I ever received. I was driven by the words that were penned by, poet, Walter Foss: *"Let me live in a house by the side of the road where the races of men go by, some who are good, some who are bad, but not as good or bad as I. I sit not in the scorners seat of hurl the cynics ban, but let me live in a house by the side of the road and be a friend to man."* That served as my charge to continue to make contributions to humanity in an effort to make our world a better place to live. I lived with the thought that I may not pass this way again; so let me give now tomorrow may never be.

As time at Wesley passed, I found myself deeply involved in choosing a project to fulfill one of the major requirements for the degree. I reflected on the murder of my beloved father in March 1978. He was slain to the best of my family's knowledge by two young black males who were under contract to silence him, because of someone's belief that he was knowledgeable of racketeering in a local hospital in New Orleans, where he served as a security guard. The fear was that he had agreed with the authorities to turn state's evidence so that prosecution would be possible for the guilty parties. We have yet to know the full truth of the matter. It is a known fact that many black- on -black crimes during that time were never fully resolved, and we are left without full closure.

The anger over my father's murder was transformed to a desire to assuage my bitter feelings by researching societal reasons for such heinous crimes against nature. It is assumed that the assailants did not know him but took his life anyway. I drew mightily on this dark experience. I went to the Alexandria, Virginia City jail and developed an initiative that turned into a full- blown mentoring program designed for young male inmates who were in need of transforming their lives. The purpose of the program was to provide guidance and direction to prison inmates who wanted to redirect their lives toward wholeness. Because of the limited moral and spiritual support programs provided to them, I felt that it would be a worthwhile contribution coming from a faith-based institution. I took my idea to the Sheriff's office, and met with Richard Ruscak, the Under Sheriff, who took my proposal to Sheriff James Dunning and Chaplain John Poffenberger. The jail officials graciously accepted the proposal.

The Alfred Street Baptist Church served as the launching pad for the newly formed Potomac Community Mentoring Program. I hand picked twenty-five male members of the church between the ages of thirty-five and fifty years of age. The criterion for selection was: college educated, high moral standards, and streetwise. All mentors were involved in a series of training seminars to acquaint them with the art of mentoring adults. The model program that was used was "Big Brothers of America" and the course of study was an inclusive curriculum led by volunteers from Prison Fellowship and a variety of clinical and professional consultants. The mentors were paired with inmates with the goal of assisting the inmate in a positive transformation from a life of crime to a productive contributor to society. The chief objective was to reduce the rate of recidivism among young black males, and to assist in bringing about a positive change in the Alexandria community. I designed the program as a model for other churches to implement. The Biblical Scripture Reference is found in Matthew 25:36c, *I was in prison and you came to visit me.*

I was able to persuade the Alexandria Office of Sheriff, and the Alexandria Adult Probation and Office Program to become partners with the Mentoring Initiative. The agreements provided a captive flow of clients for the program. The Office of Sheriff allowed the mentors to gain access to the detention facility for visits with inmates, and upon their release, the Probation and Parole Office assisted in the monitoring procedures. The success of the program was predicated on the willingness of the participants who were open to life transformation.

The Potomac Community Mentoring Program reflected the basic beliefs that every person should have an opportunity for wholesome and positive physical and social development. Within the context of the rights of individuals in the larger community, it is desirable when those who have made lawless decisions are provided the opportunities, firm support, and expectations of lawful behavior and acceptable lifestyles. I am proud of two outstanding former inmates who participated in the program, and have finished college, attended graduate school, and become mortgage brokers and novel writers. It was Jesus who said, "...I was in prison, and you came to visit me." I am happy that I go to visit those who were struggling with their lives, and looking for someone to assist them in life transformation.

This dramatic episode of my life opened a new pathway of spiritual blessings, experience with unusual people, and an opportunity to practice a social gospel. Even in a sea of despair, with hope and faith in God, mountains are passable. The Potomac Community Mentoring Program not only afforded me a closer walk with God, but also the project I used to earn my Doctorate Degree in Ministry.

My response to service to humanity has given me one of the major tenets in the purpose of the story of creation. To be called, compelled and committed summarizes our subjection to a higher order and our natural relationship to all of humanity. Do it now because you will not pass this way again.

CHAPTER IX

GO YE THEREFORE

I believed that when I accepted Jesus Christ the balance of my life would be a trouble- free journey filled with the desires of the heart. I was baptized into the Baptist faith at the age of eleven at the New Zion Baptist Church in New Orleans. I was naïve enough to believe that life would be a whole lot easier than before. I expected a complete transformation because I had begun to wear the badge of Christianity on my heart, treated others, as I wanted to be treated, attempted to adhere to the precepts of Jesus, and studied the Bible to show myself approved as one who walks with Christ. This is what I had been taught and believed as a child until the reality of life unfolded before me in the form of impaired health.

I was born with a cardiac defect with no reasonable positive outlook for a full and healthy life. I grew up in a very low-income family, experienced social rejection because of the color of my skin, and because of my color it was assumed that my life would amount to nothing. I attended an elementary school in the South where white school officials charted dual curriculums for white and black children. The curriculum for blacks was designed to prepare students for manual and domestic labor, however, the commitment of many black teachers made it possible for their students to set their sights on more challenging goals in education. My success today is the result of underpaid black teachers and white dedicated Catholic nuns who believed that I could and would accept the challenge.

I became confused early in my life when my religious teachings assured me that there is a God who dispenses love for humanity in an even-handed way, especially if you accept the path of Christianity. To this very day, the wheels of social justice continue to turn slowly, but I am called as a Christian to have unconditional faith and believe that victory comes as a gift of God. It is my faith in God that sustains me through the rigors of life.

Over the years, I have accepted that any expectation of "a better day" is here and now upon us. Studies of Holy Scriptures point to discussions on the Kingdom of God, and the benefits therein. In our limited wisdom, many of us think of the Kingdom as somewhere far beyond. The Kingdom of God is still a collection of conceptive thinking, involving the whole of our social and spiritual lives. It is not about a promise of heaven, but a transformation of life on earth into heavenly harmony. The presupposition of The Kingdom of God is the reconstruction of the life of this world, and our transforming interaction with one another toward a better good. More profoundly, building the Kingdom here on earth is our experiencing the goodness of God, and raising our appreciation to a level of witnessing that others may grow in Divine order. Building the Kingdom of God was made manifest in my life while serving as associate pastor for the Alfred Street Baptist Church congregation, and more specifically, in the ministries of pastoral counseling, chaplaincy work at the local community hospitals, the mentoring program for prison inmates, and preaching the gospel.

The preaching of the gospel became real while I was involved in those ministries. When I thought that I was fulfilling the mission that I felt called to do, God in His infinite wisdom coordinated the master plan for my life. In one of his instructional sermons, Dr. Gardner C. Taylor said, "God comes at us in such strange ways, and from such unexpected, and awkward angles." In the winter of 1996 I was at a crossroad in my ministry. I thought that I wanted to be the senior pastor of any church that would have me. After-all I was a baptized Christian, a seminary trained preacher, fortified with a multiple of religio-socio experiences, and was attempting to fill the moral and spiritual divide in the lives of the people I served. All of this was compounded by my desire to be a pastor in a church of my own.

During this time I entered a sphere of independent meditation and prayer in an attempt to ponder about the source of my downtrodden feelings. At the same time my work in organizing and coordinating the Mentoring Program, was gaining a lot of positive attention from the community as well as from my friend the late Kenneth Vallis. It was Kenneth, and John Stanford, who strongly encouraged me to pursue the Doctorate Degree in Ministry, and to extend my talents into the broader community. They were very impressed about the positive affect the mentoring program was having on the lives of the many young black jail inmates, Kenneth felt that it was worth sharing this information with the world. He shared his excitement of the program with his friend Courtland Milloy, a columnist for the *Washington Post Newspaper*, and Courtland immediately contacted me for the story. The story was a descriptive account of my life's works in the community service, and more pointedly my work in civil rights and the prison system. The title of the article was *A Captive Audience Captivated*, and ran in the paper on December 8, 1996.

Shortly after the article was circulated, I received an unusual telephone call from a man named John Jasik, program development officer of the United States Information Agency, —USIA—. John told me that he had read the Milloy column about me, and asked if I would consider serving as a U.S. Lecturer in Papua New Guinea, Vanuatu, and the Solomon Islands on the subject of "Social Change Through the use of Nonviolent Means." The American Embassy in Port Moresby, Papua New Guinea issued the original invitation. I was completely baffled, and immediately assumed that it was a joke by one of my many friends. John assured me that it was an authentic invitation, and that he would forward to me a copy of the cable of request from the American Embassy in Port Moresby. I received a copy of the cable, and discussed it with my wife and senior pastor. The article and the invitation from the USIA were unusual happenings in my life, especially when I longed for more active involvement in the gospel ministry. On January 15, 1997, I departed for Papua New Guinea, via Sydney, Australia.

I spent two days in Sydney visiting with Terry and Dian Griffiths, an Australian family that I met in the United States, and were my neighbors for four years, while serving at the Australian Embassy. It was, also, a time for reacquainting myself with Ashley, their only daughter, whom I serve as godfather. Sydney was a delightful place to visit. It would be easy for an American visitor to feel at home with the building architecture and street configuration, however the language and motorized vehicles relegated to the left side of the roadways would correct any notion of being in America. The Australian hospitality was warm and endless.

While Sydney was a wonderful stopover to visit with friends and catch up on jet lag, the voyage down under the world was now turning to the reason for my trip. As I was boarding Air New Guinea to Port Moresby, I began to wonder what was in store for me. I had never seen the natives of this foreign land, had limited knowledge of the geography, and was about to be submerged in a culture where I didn't understand the language or the culture. When the plan was airborne, I began to have anxieties about why I was even in this part of the world. What would I say to the people? How would they receive me? Is it a safe place to be? With all that was running around in my mind at thirty-six thousand feet in the air, I began to question God as to my purpose for going to this strange land. These words, found in the 28th chapter of Saint Matthew, came to my mind as clear as a bell over the roar of the racing jets: Go *ye therefore, and teach all nations, baptizing them in the name of the Father, and of the Son, and of the Holy Ghost: Teaching them to observe all things whatsoever I have commanded you: and lo, I am with you always, even unto the end of the world.* Those words were like a powerful waterfall that cleansed me of all my doubts and fears. I then knew why I was going to the South Pacific Islands. I had a story to tell, in spite of the language barrier, the difference in cultures and the socio-political climate. I was going because humanity was there awaiting my arrival.

This was one of the most liberating feelings that I had ever experienced, even compared to the cardiac surgery of 1959. I am totally convinced that God's active hand in this adventure began with my friends Kenneth Vallis and Courtland Milloy. At this lull in my ministry, I needed some reassurance that I was being used for a special purpose that could only be orchestrated by God. I knew that my prayers were being answered in a land unknown to me before. The Melanesian souls in the South Pacific needed a strong message on human relations and nonviolence as an avenue to social change. After all, history records one hundred and fifty-one years of colonization by the Dutch, Germans, Britain, Japan and Australia. The USIA, in cooperation with the Governments of Papua New Guinea, Solomon Islands and Vanuatu, arranged for me to spend appreciable time lecturing, meeting with parliaments, religious and tribal leaders, and immerse myself in the village culture. I was now ready, without reservation, to journey to Papua New Guinea.

I departed Sydney and boarded an Air New Guinea plane. At this point the journey became more serious to me than ever. As I boarded the plane, I began to wonder what Melanesian People looked like. After all, my limited knowledge of this part of the world led me to believe that the people were of olive complexion with coal black straight hair and almond eyes. The moment of truth had arrived when I observed the first airline hostess, who came to my seat to assist me. She had dark skin, short natural coarse hair, and a pleasing manner in welcoming me to Air New Guinea. After pleasant verbal exchanges, I asked if she was Melanesian, and she answered, "yes." I took a deep breath and felt that I had been initiated to the beginning of my reason for being here. When the plane landed in Port Moresby I was greeted by a host of people from the Embassy, and among them was my assigned escort, Alden P. Stallings, Public Affairs Officer. After several days in this land I found it to be raw and remarkably untamed as compared to the States. It is variegated swamp, which brought memories of the backwaters of Louisiana and Florida. The terrain composed of jagged limestone, mud and moss forest, suffocating heat, plumed birds, pearl-shelled villagers and prosaic hill people. Having not seen Melanesian people before, I thought they resembled tribes of Africa. They were quietly inquisitive of cultures that were not commonly seen on the Island, however, they were reserved, warm and quite receptive. My dark complexioned skin intrigued them, and they stared at me everywhere I went. I began to feel like a brother who had been on a long journey and had returned home. The native people were wonderfully hospitable to me. I felt an immediate kinship to the culture.

I learned that there are 750 languages in Papua New Guinea. This array of languages has made it difficult for any form of lingua franca to exist in the country. Pidgin has become the language of many, and is widely understood by the overall culture. Widespread crime remains a major factor in the capital city of Papua New Guinea, (Port Moresby). Crime involves rapes, robberies, random violence, and theft. My lodging was at Port Moresby Travelodge, where because of crime, sentries were positioned at the periphery of the hotel at all times, for the safety of the guests. It seemed that everywhere I went, I was known because of the wide press coverage that was given to the trip. The people were prepared to see the American who walked with Martin Luther King, Jr. This, to them, was tantamount to a visit into American history.

I began my days in Papua New Guinea with extensive briefings and tours by the embassy staff. The high unemployment rate was evident by the throngs of natives milling in the streets and local public parks. The high incidence of crime necessitated frequent curfews as an attempt to ensure safe streets. Observing the starkly different Melanesian culture, I wondered how I could make a positive difference in bringing them a message of human relations founded on love and respect. Their method of resolving disputes and issues is by tribal wars. During my visit, tribal war was underway on Bougainville Island. The locals were embittered by environmental destruction caused by the giant Australian-owned Panguna copper mine and by the way revenue from the mine filled a third of the national coffers but did not find its way back to their island. They formed the Bougainville Revolution Army and forced the mine to close in 1989.

The American Embassy at Port Moresby used my presence to share the late Reverend Martin Luther King's legacy of love and nonviolence through means of building peaceful relationships. My work began with the embassy staff in relating the approach to building peaceful relationships among differing cultures. The first order of business was to encourage in-depth dialogue with the people, including their social and religious heritage. The dialogue helped in understanding the values, ideologies, philosophies, and theologies of the various indigenous tribes. It was important to learn of historical colonization and their eventual independence. The information that I gained from my earlier preparation and from the embassy personnel equipped me with the knowledge to hear and address Parliament, village organizations, government workers, the legal system, the faith community, the police department, business leaders, and the penal system, Bomana Prison. The Melanesian people have an incredible respect for the civil rights work done in America by the late Reverend Martin Luther King, Jr. and his supporters. I was received like a reincarnation of Dr. King. This kind of acceptance earned me credibility so I could share techniques, methods, philosophy, and Theology that was espoused and practiced by Dr. King. Nonviolence was not the way of life in Melanesian culture. They were amazed to hear that many of America's practices were changed because of Dr. King's profound belief in the nonviolent approach to problem solving and the commitment of thousands who followed the approach. After many of my appearances, I was requested to speak to smaller organizations that were dedicated to immediate change.

My message was a simple message of harmonious approaches to human relationships for the common good. Capitalizing on the fact that the Islands were predominantly Christian, I was able to relate God's call to humanity to maintain peaceful stability by treating others as you yourself wish to be treated. The print, radio, and television media gave their undivided attention to my visit and to the message that was delivered. The Melanesian people told me that it was most unusual to have a black American come to them with such a powerful message of harmonious coexistence between tribes and cultures. After my assignment was over in Port Moresby, I journeyed with my escort to Solomon Islands.

We arrived on Solomon Islands, and were met by Keithie Saunders a strikingly tall and attractive woman with an Australian accent. Keithie served as the U.S. Consul on the Solomons. She coordinated my itinerary during my stay. The Solomons are a scattered archipelago of mountainous islands and low-lying atolls stretching from Bougainville Island to Vanuatu located about 1780m northeast of Australia. These islands became a fully –independent state and member of the Commonwealth in 1978. The government is a constitutional monarchy with the British monarch as head of state. The Solomons are occupied primarily by Melanesians who struggle with the same social and unemployment issues as Papua New Guinea. I found the population to be friendly and less threatening than Papua New Guinea. My initial attention was drawn to the people I observed with natural red and blond hair, and black skin. In my interactions, I learned that English was the official language, which made my visit easier and my message understandable. The Solomon Islanders were most interested in what I had to share about nonviolence improving human relations within tribes and with Australia and New Zealand. Almost 95% of the Solomon Islanders were Christian, which made my message of nonviolence toward social and economic change acceptable.

My visit provided me the opportunity to address the deputy prime minister, governor general, minister of Education, police commissioner, banking officials, the faith community, and members of Parliament. These were the people and disciplines with the influence and followers to effect positive change.

I also spent a considerable amount of time visiting the villages of the poor and disenfranchised, with a special interest in the education and development of youth. Many of the villages were true examples of social and economic deprivation. I saw scores of children without the nurture and care of the nuclear family structure, and meager resources for daily survival. I had the opportunity to learn that some degree of cannibalism was still being practiced among people who were living outside of Christianity. While this culture was alien to me, I recognized that they are part of the story of human creation, and needed the care and support of their fellow human beings. My interest was to provide models of human survival in the transforming theatre of protest culminating in positive action. I made my observations known to the U.S. Embassy and they hung on to every word. The native people were more concerned about how the American civil rights movement was able to attract large numbers of people, i.e., the March on Washington, D.C. in 1963. It was easy to explain that when the masses have common issues and a single enemy, the mobilization of people becomes less of a problem.

While the issue of crime on the Solomons was less than on Papua New Guinea, I was invited to the sole prison on the Island. The prison was primitive, and policed by a small ill-trained military contingent of uniformed soldiers. I was welcomed to talk to them about the inmate-mentoring program that I established in the United States. The prison administration was eager to learn how the Solomon Islands faith community could adapt the mentoring concept for their inmates. It was gratifying to share an idea that has proven to transform people. Through an interpreter, I had one-on-one conversations with inmates. I shared positive experiences of other individuals who survived similar fates. I used this opportunity to encourage the men to be open to the acceptance of positive role models in their lives. This act of compassion served as an extension of my Christian ministry in the U. S. I learned from this encounter with the imprisoned men of the Solomons that the overall character and behavior of humanity is similar, and needs the attention from good neighbors regardless of culture or race.

When my work was completed in the Solomons, my escort and I journeyed to an Island in the southwest pacific called Vanuatu. This beautiful stretch of land is part of a "Y" shaped configuration of 83 islands that are densely forested with floral beauty. We arrived in the mid-afternoon on Quantas Airline to discover a welcoming party of delightful happy people who decorated us with colorful leis around our necks. I was so astonished with the tropical weather and the beauty of the landscape, I telephoned my wife and told her to sell our house in the states immediately and come and join me in paradise. Ninety-four per cent of the population is made up of indigenous Melanesians. Small minorities of Chinese, Fijians, Vietnamese, Tongans, and Europeans account for the balance. Vanuatu is a parliamentary democracy. Britain and France were granted Independence on July 30, 1980, after 74 years of joint rule. Prior to independence the country was known as New Hebrides. I was invited to this country to share in lectures and comparative dialogue on the value and adjustment under their relatively new independence. There were new behaviors to be learned and observed which were parallel to similar legislative changes that took place in America pursuant to the civil rights movement.

My contributions were well received by the Parliament and the people of Vanuatu. They welcomed me to speak in their places of worship, and to smaller interest groups. As this tour of three Melanesian countries came to an end, the reason for the junket became clearer to me. The people were undergoing a new way of life, and experiencing a new type of governance that made them responsible for its success. They had trust in the universal principles that brought about a fundamental transformation of race relations within the United States under the leadership of Dr. King. My role with Dr. King was close enough to him to share his theological and philosophical approach to social change using the methods of nonviolence. While their traditional approach to settling often involved violence, I was able to draw their attention to a more peaceful way to dialogue and prolong life. This was one of my biggest challenges, especially dealing with a population of people who were unaccustomed to nonviolence. I long to return to the Pacific to evaluate my affect on the thinking of the people.

One of many differences between the Melanesians and black Americans was the problem of communication. Papua New Guinea alone hosted over 800 distinct languages and was divided into hundreds of clans. These divisions, compounded by ethnic differences and a long history of inter-clan conflict, seriously impeded Government efforts to provide services under equal treatment. My journey was to have them do an introspective examination of themselves as they were undergoing social change in a shared organizational construct. There were familiar similarities to America, in the gross unemployment of young Melanesian males who had drifted from rural to urban areas looking for employment opportunities. Many of these young men became frustrated with the lack of job opportunities and resorted to violence to provide for themselves and their relatives. Bomana Prison is overflowing with wayward men who struggle with living in squalor, with no visible positive resources in the future. It has been, and still remains, my attempt to take Dr. King's message to as many areas of the world as possible to bring a new and fresh meaning to nonviolence as an agent to social change.

CHAPTER X

CALL TO COMMUNITY

In August of 1997, I took a position with the Alexandria city government as special assistant to the city manager/director of human relations. During this period, Vola Lawson served as city manager. She was well known for her warm manner of human relations, and good government. Vola began her tenure in Alexandria's city government as the director of housing programs, and gained notoriety in the dispensation of her duties. When I entered the employ of the Alexandria city government, I had a single agenda, which was citywide unification. The city's 1990 census accounted for a population of 110,000 people, and I believed that a city of that size with goodwill could unite and become a model for America.

Prior to my employment in the City Government, a mutual friend, Ferdinand Day, who thought that I could make a positive contribution to the city, introduced me to Vola. When the position of special Assistant came available, I applied and was selected. The job included the Office on Human Rights, the Office on Women, Affirmative Action, and special duties involving troubleshooting issues of race and culture. I managed approximately 25 people who wanted to be advocates for social change. With my background of fighting for justice within the ranks of the civil rights movement, the position was tailor made for me. The position came during unsettling days for me at Alfred Street Baptist Church. I was in dire need of an opportunity to assist in the education and social resource development of Alexandria. This interest was not at Alfred Street at the time. The church was not known for community outreach or embracing those in need, unless they were bonafide members of the church. There was a standing rule that needy persons who came to the church for money, food or clothing were to be directed to other social programs of the city for assistance. Alfred Street suffered the reputation of an exclusive church indifferent to the down and out. I found difficulty serving in a faith community that handed turkeys to the poor at Thanksgiving and then left them to fend for their lives during the balance of the year.

The spirit of the Civil Rights Movement was driving my life, which was my motivating force for addressing many of the social ills that plagued the lives of those who had no voice in their destiny. Vola Lawson was an advocate for justice and equality and finding wrong, and making it right. We understood one another, and had much in common. We are close in age, love movies, and we are from the South, which make us sympathetic to those who struggle against the odds.

My job with the City provided me with the opportunity to see the deprivation of the homeless, the hungry, the jobless, and the children who were at odds with the educational system, and struggling for a balanced education. Because of Vola's supportive commitment, I could be creative in the coordination of City services to the needy, bring about peace and understanding in situations of discontent. We endured a period of time when some students from the City's single public high school were embroiled in violent behavior at weekend social gatherings. Their behavior spilled over into the school the following week. Vola asked me to go to the school and develop a creative way to bring an end to the disruptive violent behavior that had become disruptive. I carefully and quickly assessed the situation and developed an effective program on anger management called "CHOICES." The principal for students who were involved in questionable behavior mandated this program. It dealt with the student reviewing his or her unacceptable actions with a counselor, and making corrective choices toward improving interpersonal communication and relationships with other students. CHOICES was a dialogue method between students of differing factions outside of the normal classroom setting. Reginald "Asante" Clark, a group dynamics leader and program leader in the Department of Human Services at the Northern Virginia Community College in Alexandria provided me assistance. Asante and I made a compatible team, and helped many students reflect on their behavior and make the transformation into an acceptable lifestyle. The program lasted two years with lasting good results. The CHOICES program provided a non-threatening challenge to making positive decisions in resolving of conflicts. When our youth are presented with alternative options to violence, we move in the right direction to build safer communities.

Some perceive Alexandria as a city with good relationships across racial and cultural lines; however, many relationships were superficial and tolerated at best. Until 1970, there were no black elected officials, Ira Robinson was elected as the first black city Council member with impressive white support. During Robinson's tenure, Ferdinand Day was appointed as the first black person to the Alexandria City School Board. These two political actions gave some assurance that Alexandria's black citizens were entering city-wide policy level positions that provided nontraditional representation for the underprivileged.

Since 1970 the city has seen a small number of black people elected to city council, school board, and appointed to boards and commissions but not nearly representative of the black population of the city. In 1975, local black attorney Melvin Miller ran for mayor, and only garnered a minimal number of the city's voting populous. This sent a signal that Alexandria was not ready for black mayoral leadership. Melvin and I worked together at the D.C. Redevelopment Land Agency in Washington, D.C. He was the director of development for RLA. He came with a great degree of knowledge of the field of development— however, he had a strong interest in politics, and moved in political circles in Alexandria. He thought he had earned the favor of the voters, but sadly came to the realization that his time had not arrived nor had the city become racially impartial. During his campaign he requested his long time friend, Wiley Mitchell to give his campaign a boost by consenting to have a photograph taken with him. It was reported that Mitchell responded to Melvin that he could not do that, even though Melvin worked to get Mitchell elected to the senate in the state legislature. The rejection received by Melvin from Mitchell was a serious fracture to the tenuous relationships between races in the city of Alexandria. However, twenty-eight years later Alexandria elected William D. Euille as its first black mayor. While it seems that progress is in the making, it has been a long time coming. This blatant example of the past imbalance between what appeared, on surface, to be an equitable relationship was deceptive and unacceptable. The result of this incident became the talk of the black community accompanied by an attitude of mistrust, and the need to unify on all fronts. Blacks began to organize in voting blocks in an effort to support the candidates of their choice. Black churches gave their support in allowing candidates to campaign in their congregations. The City became highly racially polarized by Alexandria standards

In 1997 two members of the Alexandria City Council—William Euille, Vice Mayor and Lonnie Rich, councilman— proposed an initiative called "Call to Community," that would celebrate the diversity of races and cultures by coming together in positive dialogue. As many cities on the American continent, Alexandria's demographics were undergoing dramatic global change. The City was approaching a problem of racial and cultural diversity that was a new experience for all concerned. Over the years, the issues between black and white people had not been resolved, and with the influx the city recognized Hispanics, Asians, Africans, and other cultures from around the world the city recognized that we needed to build relationships between all groups to ensure good relations, and a safer community. In 1998 the City Council adopted Resolution No. 1858, which endorsed the initiation of the Call to Community Program. While the program's sponsors were members of the council, it was consistent with President Clinton's national initiative to explore dialogue on issues concerning race and culture. The resolution authorized Vice Mayor Euille and Council Member Rich to plan the City's Call to Community Program. The Steering Committee adopted the following mission statement:

The purpose of the Alexandria Call to Community Steering

Committee was to promote racial harmony and cultural understanding among all Alexandrians.

The Call to Community Steering Committee developed a Plan of Action and formed two subcommittees—Kickoff Event Subcommittee and Neighborhood Forums Subcommittee. The Kickoff Event Subcommittee was responsible for organizing and launching the first Call to Community Program—which involved publicity, location, a keynote speaker and a panel of speakers to lead audience participation. The Neighborhood Forums Subcommittee was to organize local forums on a neighborhood level, identify facilitators, a location, and provide publicity. Several other subcommittees were developed, including Community Forums, Honest Brokers, and Projects. I was requested by the city manager to serve as the staff coordinator of Call to Community which involved organizing steering committee meetings, working with community organizations in the planning and the execution of dialogue forums, media coverage, soliciting and maintaining a multicultural speakers bureau. After many weeks of media coverage, on November 8, 1998, the Call to Community Program kick-off event was held at the George Washington National Masonic Memorial with a standing- room- only crowd. It was reassuring to have such demonstrated interest in promoting unity in this historical slave-auctioning city. After the initial meeting, where plans were made to continue examining racial and cultural relations, several neighborhood forums were held, which eventually lost momentum because of indecisive leadership by the steering committee brought on by intra-organizational conflict.

Out of frustration and the need to regenerate momentum, I founded the Alexandria Student Forum in 1999 as an adjunct initiative under the umbrella of the Call to Community. The Student Forum evolved from eight Alexandria public and private middle and high schools, and is a special program for school youth who are interested in working toward a better understanding of the different races and cultures in their community. It is an initiative that responds to the need to enhance better communications between students of different races and cultures. The goals were to identify and develop solutions for coming together. This was to be accomplished through community dialogue that enhances relationships between diverse races and cultures. This was a venture based on faith and the goodwill of interested students who were dedicated to making a positive change in the Alexandria Community.

Unlike adults, the students were not reticent in discussing racial and cultural matters that impeded progress in relationships. The Student Forums, under my guidance, were planned by a small and dedicated planning committee of students from the participating schools, and sponsored by the Alexandria City Council, the Alexandria City Public School Board, and a federation of private school representatives. The faculty and students at the Episcopal High School Field House with 1,000 students hosted the first forum in attendance. Jack Moline Rabbi of Agudas Achim Hebrew Congregation responded positively to my request to serve as the first facilitator. Rabbi Moline was a natural group dynamics leader, and led the students in meaningful dialogue on the sensitive issues of race and culture.

The Student Forum was such a mammoth success, as told by the student participants, "this experience was more meaningful than the traditional classroom setting of an administratively chosen curriculum." They were free to discuss issues of racial and cultural divides that were not discussed in their homes or other places of assembly. This forum presented a new arena for open discussion about race relations that were normally avoided. The students faced these troubling issues far better than the adults in the Call to Community initiative. Since 1999, I have conducted more successful student forums in the cities of Richmond and Alexandria, Virginia. I plan to introduce every major American Urban Center to the idea. The resounding spirit of the Student Forum is to keep the dream of freedom alive and active until every vestige of segregation is buried in loving relationships of peace and unity. It is an approach to normal interactive relationships between students of goodwill, and builds bridges to connect the divides. Experience teaches that youth are not reticent about discussing sensitive issues such as race and culture. This approach assures a positive community building process.

CHAPTER XI

IN SEARCH OF UNITY

One of the poetic Psalms of David reminds us, "How good and how pleasant it is for brothers to live together in unity." He likens this harmonious and unified living to the precious oil that was poured on Aaron's head at his anointing by Moses when Aaron became the first High Priest. The oil saturated his beard, and ran down to the collar of his robe. It was as the dew of Mount Harmon, reported as the highest mountain in the vicinity of Palestine, was falling on Mount Zion, which was the City of David. The writer provides us with a sense of completeness in unity. David inspired this meaningful thought. His life, though God loved him, was fraught with pain, violence, deception, and division. He experienced what division can do to bring the demise of a people, and certainly to an individual's soul. Through his trials, he never forgot to keep God at the very center of his life. He grew to know that in unity there is strength. Unity has served as the staying power in life's struggles. When Jesus lamented about his eminent death, He prayed a prayer of unifying all believers, (John 17:23), "Father I in them and you in me. May they be brought to complete unity to let the world know that you sent me and have loved them, even as you have loved me." The order of Divine creation was done with the intent that we would live together and bear each other's burdens, but we have found ourselves in a quandary of divisiveness with little or no respect, no caring, no feeling for our fellow beings. We are often caught up in selfishness and greed.

In my constant quest for a less divided human community, I continue to have faith that there are more people of good will than not, however, they appear to be much too silent on the issues that unify us. We are living in a time where we are experiencing more isolation from one another than ever before. In his encouragement of unity among humanity, John Donne's poem, *"No Man Is An Island,"* should heighten our awareness to the fact that none of us can rise to our fullest potential entirely unto ourselves: so says Donne:

*NO MAN IS AN ISLAND ENTIRE OF ITSELF
EVERY MAN IS A PIECE OF THE CONTINENT,
A PART OF THE MAIN...ANY MAN'S DEATH
DIMINISHES ME, BECAUSE I AM INVOLVED IN
MANKIND: AND THEREFORE NEVER SEND
TO KNOW FOR WHOM THE BELL TOLLS; IT
TOLLS FOR THEE.*

The bell is tolling for us to answer the call to community, even with our differences. Our lives should be oriented to building community together, a community of love, trust and faith in the ability to see the good in humanity. Together, we can create a community that our children will find merit in, and will want to emulate. Positive models are necessary and important for children. If a child lives in a community without respect for people, he will be disrespectful of others. If a child lives in an unconnected community of division and hate, he will live a life of confusion and violence. If a child lives in a diverse community where cultures are positively celebrated, he will experience the wholeness of life that God intended.

During the 1960s I served as a principal participant in the civil rights movement, and was privileged to witness a preview of what is possible when diverse people of color, race and culture come together and agree on a positive cause. Unity is what God has provided for us to live in love, peace, and harmony, regardless of the views we have about others who don't look like us, or speak as we do, or act as we act. It doesn't matter how we have made false judgments about each other, there comes a time when we should come to recognize the intrinsic good in all of us, and rise to the occasion of extending brotherly and sisterly love to the abused, the misused, the forgotten, and the downtrodden. In our search for unity we will find its deepest roots in our spiritual nature. In the book of Acts 10:34, it is recorded that *God is no respecter of persons.*

Biblical historians identify Simon Peter as a devout Jew who believed that salvation was only for the Jews. He experienced a stark revelation from God's Holy Spirit when he was led to the home of a Gentile named Cornelius. He was in doubt as to whether he was within the realm of Jewish law as he stood in the company of Gentiles, Gentiles were perceived to be different. They spoke different, they looked different—and after all, they were not Jewish. However, it was made known to Peter in a vision that God is God to the Jew, the Greek, the Nubian, the Samaritan, and the whole of humankind.

When I served as a principal participant in the great civil rights Movement of the 1950s and 1960s, I was privileged to be an eyewitness to what is possible when people of color, race and culture agree on a positive and common cause. There is something that is very liberating about unity. I remember the story of an elderly black woman who had set her aged feet to the hot roads of the south in a demonstration for freedom. She was asked by a news reporter if she was tired of walking, and she replied, **"Son, my feets is tired, but my soul is rested, "cause we is walking to freedom."** Liberation is a point of agreement with all people who have been oppressed. After taking an introspective look at the stereotypical views that we have had about others who do not look like us, or speak as we do, or act as we do, we need to understand what it is like to be in another's shoes. Even though we may falsely judge others, there is an intrinsic good in all of us. Its deepest roots are spiritual, in nature. When spiritual roots connect a community, it is transformed to beautiful spiritual roots of the struggle it is transformed from the jangling discords of time to a beautiful symphony of peace and tranquility with a desire for unity. Because of our differences in nature, living in harmony does not mean that we will always be in total agreement. Differing opinions are important in the equation of life when attempting to reach consensus. We should agree on our purpose to work together for the common good with our outward expressions revealing our inward unity of purpose.

CHAPTER XII

OVERCOMING REJECTION

⋆⇌⇋⋆

There was a time early in my ministry that I wanted desperately to be the pastor of any church. All of my ministerial models were pastors with great followings. In addition to the popularity that comes with such a calling, I felt that I needed a base of operations for my special calling to a social gospel. The late Reverend Dr. Martin Luther King, Jr. had exhibited the persona and image I admired and wanted to emulate. There were others who had the gifts and the calling to impressive congregations, such as Dr. Gardner C. Taylor, a great orator and pastor emeritus of Concord Baptist Church, in Brooklyn, New York, Dr. William Augustus Jones, pastor of Bethany Baptist Church, in Brooklyn, New York, the late Dr. A.L. Davis, Jr. pastor of New Zion Baptist Church in New Orleans, Louisiana, the late Dr. Samuel DeWitt Proctor, pastor of Abyssinian Baptist Church in New York, and many others who have made great socio/religio contributions. I felt it necessary to prepare myself in advance of any calling to a pulpit. I attended two seminaries and attained the degree of Doctor of Ministry. I was cited as doing outstanding work while studying. I served as an effective pastoral counselor for many subjects regarding life issues. I spent much time in tearful prayer asking God to release me to be a pastor, and I was denied by one church after another.

Whenever I would apply to a church, I would inevitably receive a letter denying my application after calling another candidate. One church requested that my wife be interviewed by their pulpit committee for reasons that are unknown by us. We thought her interview was a bit unusual, especially since I was under consideration to be the pastor. Eventually, I learned from a reliable source that I was denied the pastorate because my wife is caucasian. I was never told by the pulpit committee why I was rejected. My naïve mind questioned such a decision by Christian people. I continued my research into past decisions by churches that rejected me; I ascertained that there was pervasive prejudice in many black churches against having a white woman as "first lady" of the church. . My qualifications for the pastorate did not seem to be at issue. Whether I was able to teach and lead them in the knowledge contained in the Holy Scriptures was inconsequential. It did not seem to matter that my wife and I spent years on the front lines of the Civil Rights Movement demonstrating for equal rights for all citizens. It did not even seem to matter that my wife and I are followers of Jesus Christ. What mattered to us was that we followed God's sacrament of holy matrimony across racial lines, and have raised three healthy, independent God- fearing children who are well grounded in the principles of faith, fairness and equity.

Another reason that comes to mind about my pastoral rejection theory is my attitude and practice of dramatics and entertainment in the pulpit. I remain convinced that many black congregations choose their pastors on how well they entertain churchgoers. During one segment of the pastoral selection process, the pulpit committee requests that each candidate preach one or several sermons to give the congregation a legitimate feel for the candidate's oratory gifts. If the preacher arouses enough emotions, he or she is given a very high rating for further consideration. I was not called to entertain, but to lead and to teach by example. In many cases there is no judgment of qualifications for the teaching and interpretation of the Bible, Church Administration, pastoral counseling or effectiveness in social concerns. The absence of such concerns has given rise to many failed churches that eventually request pastoral resignations; which cause repercussions in the surrounding community. In days and years past, the church was once known as the very center of community life where the pastor was resourceful and knowledgeable in the support of lost and needy sheep of the church family and community. While many churches are fulfilling God's call to service, others have become for- profit businesses.

Much time has passed since I lamented about being rejected as a pastor, and I have come full circle in recognizing that God's call on my life may never be fully understood by the mere mortal mind, but I have come to a point of full satisfaction in my journey of service to God. In chapter IX, I cite the clear revelation of my purpose, as I understand my mission according to Saint Matthew 28:19, 20. I am totally satisfied being God's contagious spiritual gadfly modeling the spirit of hope, joy, forgiveness and peace. I have come to complete acceptance of whatever God's will is for me. I will forever find satisfaction, and do His will. In the will of God, man's rejection of me is not a factor as to whether I ascend to victory or suffer defeat, but whether I please God in my daily living.

I declare victory when I sit on a sleeping cot with an inmate in some dingy jail and bring hope of transformation of a positive life to him or her, and they find reason to envision a brighter day. Victory is mine when an elderly person who is confined to a dismal institution asks me to read God's redeeming word for blessed assurance. I see victory through my tears of joy when the physically and spiritually infirmed are healed as a result of my concentrated prayers to a God who is not acquainted with defeat.

Success to man is transforming what appears to be adversity into those things that we deem rewarding and satisfying. I believe there is divine order under which we live, and are governed by. What we view as defeat, failure or rejection could very well be the result of pursuing a path that God's has planned for our lives. My efforts to become a pastor could be seen as God's way of guiding me to broader fields of ministry where I have been used to spiritually affect more lives beyond an organized congregation. In the fulfillment of my ministry I continue to minister to those who are incarcerated in jails, patients in mental asylums and hospitals, and the socially and economically indigent, and I continue preaching the good news of the gospel all over the world. I have learned that if one is called to be an earnest leader, he or she must learn to be a servant, — for Servant hood is synonymous to victory.

I Shall Not Pass This Way Again

In my study of the biblical account of the rebuilding of Jerusalem's wall by Nehemiah, I was encouraged by his commitment and dedication to reconstruct a meaningful functioning monument that became a major part of Jewish history. In spite of the criticism, death threats, and rejection he received from his enemies, under his leadership the wall was restored. Likewise, David was discouraged and sought by envious Saul. However, he persevered and became King David. He refused to succumb to rejection. The historical accounts of human survival serve as a guide t living victoriously, in spite of the obstacles. I take my hope from the lyrics of the old Negro Spiritual*: A'm so glad dat trouble don' lass always.*

In many cases, rejections are based on inconclusive observations of what appears to be fact. Usually decisions to reject are based on fragments of the whole, and not on total fact. Surface assumptions are made by what one sees on the surface. We observe outward behavior without insight into the cause of the behavior. Basically, we act on the basis of what we see, and not what we know.

During my years of social and educational development, I doubted myself as an outstanding or even acceptable student. I was always at the bottom rung of the social and educational ladder. I was small for my age, and not athletically developed, therefore, while other boys excelled in sports, I usually stood on the sidelines, and made excuses about not wanting to participate. When I did attempt to participate, I felt that I made a fool of myself. Because of my inability to compete with others, I was very often rejected when teammates were chosen. The very nature of the male species is to be competitive, in sports, and I was usually left out because I was not. After many years through elementary school, it became clear to me that I was not the athletic type. Because of constant rejections, my interest was dissipated and drowned in self-defeat. The time had come to choose extra-curricular activities that would boast in my low self-esteem.

In elementary school, the faculty combined their talents and produced musical festivals each year. The call went out for student volunteers to showcase their talents in becoming festival participants. I remember being reticent about volunteering, because I was under the impression that my parents could not afford the cost of costumes, and other props. Being sensitive about our family finances, and the fear of suffering rejection, I did not volunteer. When my mother learned that I held back because of the fear of not having adequate finances, she admonished me by telling me to leave the concern about finances to my father and her, and inform the teachers that I will participate. My mother's support changed my feelings of inadequacy and the fear of rejection. As long as my parents were with me, I had the will and desire to do anything, and with confidence. My interest for the stage deepened, and I became accomplished in whatever role I was given.

These earlier rejections prepared me for future adverse ordeals, which are integral parts in the process of maturing. Our gifts of talents are varied and different from one another, and it is up to each of us to find where we excel. Accept rejection as a wake up call to your true calling. In the words of Anais Nin, "Beware of allowing a tactless word, a rebuttal, a rejection to obliterate the whole sky."[1] As a black man in America, rejection continues to be a definitive way of life, but with one redeeming feature, which is the innate comfort of my durable existence to resurface another day and defeat the barriers of yesterday.

CHAPTER XIII

FEAR IN TIMES OF UNCERTAINTY

Until my father died I lived with fear of the unknown, fear of failing, and fear of not being allowed to develop to my fullest potential. My father was taken away from us, without warning, by a murderer's weapon. It became clear to me on the plane ride to New Orleans for the funeral that there are no guarantees for the future, therefore every day of life could be the last. Fear of the known and the unknown is a natural phenomenon in our lives. We become anxious about things that we know will hurt us, and we become alarmed about the evils in the unknown that we perceive will harm us. As a child, I experienced fear of the dark because I could not discern what I could not see. My imagination took flight and caused me to conjure every manner of evil in the dark I feared the ferocity of unfamiliar barking dogs that I felt could do me harm. I, also, feared the reprimands of my parents when I disobeyed them. Experiencing fear is nature's way of alerting us to the possibilities of evil and pain.

Sigmund Freud, the Austrian neurologist and founder of psychoanalysis, spoke of someone who was quite properly afraid of snakes in the heart of the African jungle, and another person who neurotically feared that snakes were under the carpet in his house. Freud said that many fears are real, and others are acquired. Most fears are snakes under the carpet. During the time of America's most memorable economic depression and wars, Franklin Delano Roosevelt, the 32nd U.S.President uttered these words in his inaugural address: *We have nothing to fear but fear itself.*

Fear has always been an important factor in human survival. We are now threatened with the complete destruction, and annihilation of the human race. The world is on edge because of nuclear threats, and trigger-happy world leaders. We can look back over the past few decades when our politicians promised a brighter future with a flourishing economy and improved relationships between races and cultures. Unfortunately, because of greed, hate and racism, the world community has been reduced to fear on every continent. The clouds of destruction differ from one continent to another, but the global concern is fear. We would be better served to leave our nagging fears behind, and focus on our dreams of a secure future— where all can thrive and be all God intends. Many of us have become too focused on ourselves, and have slowly lost our sense of community whether in our immediate neighborhoods, our nation, or the world. We no longer consider the needs of those constantly living with fear. Terrorism, disease, pesticides, and the eroding environment compound our fears. Our lives have gone through drastic changes since the September 11, 2001 tragedy. We have become afraid of large public gatherings, the water we drink, the food we eat, the air we breathe, and the strangers that we meet who don't look and talk as we do. No nation has the right to believe that the world belongs solely to them, nor should they believe that they have bona-fide rights to all of the resources therein. It has been alleged that the arrogance of America sends a perceived message throughout the world that we believe we are the supreme rulers of the world. The scriptures in the 24th Psalm state that, " The Earth is the Lord's, and the fullness therein…"

We are living in an age of fear, depression, and despair— an age when we overlook common sense and reasoning. Instead of a constant quest for a peaceful and harmonious world, we invest our resources in the military industrial complex, which we think can maintain peace. Fear has supplanted our reliance on sound and equitable judgment. In David's penmanship of the 23rd Psalm, he speaks of his own experience with fear in trying times. He says, *yea though I walk through the valley of the shadow of death, I will fear no evil: For thou art with me; Thy rod and thy staff they comfort me...* In David's mortal response to his many close calls with death, he kept God at the center of his life. The very thought of death causes our internal response to be fear which casts a frightening shadow over our being. In combating fear, I am often reminded of the words of the song writer, Thomas Dorsey, *Like a ship that's tossed and driven, battered by angry sea, when the storms of life are raging and the fury falls on me, I wonder what I have done that makes this race so hard to run, then I say to my soul, take courage The Lord will make a way somehow.*

There is a word in the book of John, (6:5-13), that talks about what Jesus can do with what seems to be impossible situations. The story presents a teaming multitude of people who were in a damnable religio-socio predicament. They had been following and listening to the sermons of Jesus over the period of a long day. They were hungry, but they were afraid that there was no— food, and especially for such a large crowd. Biblical history teaches us that God comes at us in many different ways. Through Jesus, a little boy surrenders his meager lunch of two fish and five barley loaves. From this little lunch, Jesus performed a miracle of expansion to feed 5,000 hungry people until their appetites were satisfied. It is believed that Jesus was able to do this, because the little boy gave the lunch from his hands to the hands of Jesus. As for fear, I believe that when you give your fears over to the hands of Jesus He can do more with it in his hands than you can do with it in your hands.

Unconditional faith in God's ability to transform adversities into victories is my approach to overcoming fear. I withdraw from the busy world of competing dynamics and spend time in thoughtful solitude, and prayer, focusing on three basic tenants of *believing, yielding,* and *committing.* These three approaches to Godly success are the prominent landmarks on the journey toward peace and salvation. When one becomes a believer, all fears and doubts are erased. Faith becomes the pathway to the object or goal of the believer. When one is a believer, he or she becomes saturated with the gift of the Holy Spirit, and claims the good news that is about to happen before it happens. *Believing* is reconciling all that has happened before, and graciously accepting that which is to come. *Yielding* is losing one's self in total surrender to God, and entrusting your fears in the hands of the assured deliverer. When one yields, surrender of the total self becomes the fulfillment of the essence of life. In yielding, you can find new meaning in the hymn; *Jesus is all the world to me, my life, my joy, my all. He is my strength from day to day. Without Him I would fall. When I am sad to Him I go, no other one can cheer me so. When I am sad He makes me glad...He's my friend*

Commitment is related to yielding. When one makes a faith commitment, he or she enters into a binding and pledged relationship with God. A relationship that is promised to endure in the good and not so good times. To commit is a faith marriage to truth, and devotion. While passing through this fearful sphere of my life, when nations exist in distrust of one another, and the decisions of world politicians are born out of greed and the desire for personal power, I am directed to the passage of scripture that places mankind in proper position. Psalm 8:6, states that God intended for man to have complete authority over the earth. With such authority comes the sense of knowing from whence the authority comes, and keen observation, and adherence to the limits to be exercised. In the rearing of our children, as parents, we have the authority to do what we wish, but we also have the responsibility to nurture, feed, and care for them in well being or sickness. In my quest to understand more of what God's will is for me, I continue to return to an unconditional faith that allows me to live on the gift of His grace, without fear of any kind, and with the realization that I am in His constant care. I am convinced that the reason we find fear difficult to overcome is our inability to trust that God is the sovereign authority who is in undisputable control of the universe. Again, I left my fear in the cabin of an airplane en-route to my father's funeral in New Orleans.

CHAPTER XIV

RELENTLESS PURSUIT

In my life, I have learned that anything worthwhile is worth pursuing. I came to the conclusion in my early adulthood that success comes in"cans", and not "cants". When I relocated to teach school in Chicago, I was refused employment because of a malfunctioning heart. Before I reached adulthood, my parents were asked to sign a medical permission form giving consent to the surgeons to correct my cardiac problem, because of their lack of confidence in medical technology, they refused to sign. The opportunity that was presented by the doctors never left my mind, so I remained patient until I was of age to sign for myself. Today, I am cured. The only way I could do that was my undiluted faith in the mercy of God, and my tenacious ability to press on to the goal of having the problem corrected. Real victory comes as the result of commitment, and dedication to a specific goal. A goal that is not obstructed by our inability to persevere. If we believe that what we are going after is worth pursuing, then nothing should deter or dissuade us from obtaining it.

In the wide world of sports we are often reminded that there is a winner and a loser. More precisely, it is the thrill of victory or the agony of defeat. It is the diligence and perseverance of the contestants that make them willing to chance the possibility of being victorious. A successful runner is taught to never look back, when in pursuit of the goal, but to run the race with confidence, thrusting the body forward and pressing on to the goal, which is always ahead.

During the summer of 1990, I stood in the Olympic Stadium in Seoul, Korea among some 10,000 people from all over the world. We sang "All Hail The Power Of Jesus Name," in a demonstration of confidence in our meeting. I thought of a runner by the name of Carl Lewis. Lewis represented the United States of America just two years before, as he won the gold medal in his record-breaking speed. He pressed on to the thrill of victory. It is important to have goals in life. It is better to fail with a goal than to succeed without one. If we succeed without a goal we won't know what to do after getting there. If one has a goal, even if it has not been reached, there is a sense of direction and purpose in one's life.

I live by the thought that my greatest days are before me, not behind. I have never been able to achieve anything by holding on to the past. I view the past as a milestone by which I measure how far I have come. I could never see it as a millstone holding me back. The good old days are wonderful for reasons of experience and history, but my hunger for the unexplored keeps me pressing forward to new goals. I have come to frame my life like the long distance runner. It is not an easy run; it is strenuous; calling for physical and mental endurance, with a dedication to discipline. There have been times that impediments have blocked my way, which makes the race hard to run, but a well ordered discipline overrides life's hurdles. It is easy to resort to anger when someone crosses your path without warning. It is easy to quit when things don't go your way. It is easy to blame others when the fault is our own. Thanks be to God, there is added power, strength, and grace to anyone who keeps the faith. Given certain adverse trials in my life, I have learned how to transform what appears to be defeating agony into the thrill of victory, and it is born out of the will to "press on" in spite of obstacles.

> *Sometimes the way gets very dark, but I press on, Sometimes the hills become very steep, but I press on, sometimes great storm clouds gather over my pathway, but I press on, sometimes friends mistreat me, but I press on, sometimes I feel discouraged, and*

feel my mortal weakness overtake me, but I press on.
If I fall, I get up, and endure to the end.
Gardner C. Taylor

In the words of an unknown soul who felt the presence of the Lord always abiding in his life:

> I have seen the lightning flashing
> I have heard the thunder roll
> I have felt sin breakers dashing
> Which tried to conquer my soul;
> I've heard the voice of my savior
> He bid me still fight on.
> He promised never to leave me alone.

It is a comforting thought to have unconditional faith when you attempt to solve life's many problems, you are never alone. We just need to acknowledge it while being assured.

CHAPTER XV

LET THE CHURCH BE THE CHURCH

I have revered and respected the Black Church for as long as I can remember. My family roots are anchored in the church and its teachings. I grew up in a family where church was regarded as the place where God presides, and if you were outside of that realm of thinking something bad would overcome you. Church was the very center of my developing experience. My earliest memory was my attending Sunday school at New Mount Zion Baptist Church in Jackson, Mississippi. I recall my first vocal solo; *Yes Jesus Loves Me*, and my first exposure to reciting Bible verses. My parents insisted that I have an active part in my religious development. I was involved in the children's choir, Baptist training Union— BTU— seasonal religious plays, and Daily Vacation Bible School.

After we relocated to New Orleans, my parents assumed membership in the New Zion Baptist Church where my father became an usher, and eventually a deacon. On my eleventh birthday I was baptized, received as a full member, and continued church activities until my junior year in high school. Then I began to explore other church options that went beyond the physical emotions of people. When I was a child, the black church experience for me was an all day Sunday gathering of dismal- looking people who feared God, and a preacher who stood in the pulpit and told us all the things that we should not do. It appeared that ministers would use the time of worship to admonish their members for wanting a better life here on earth. There seemed to be very little hope for the down and out. Many of the ministers were uneducated, but talented in drawing out emotions. There had to be a better church experience of church than the one that I was having. Without denying my Afro-centric heritage, I felt the need to search for a different church experience.

My boyhood friend, Herbert Jackson, and I, with the consent of our parents, began to attend the Central Congregational Church, where there appeared to be a more educated membership who was prone to a sophisticated worship, with less emphasis on emotions. Central was a church made up of what appeared to be the New Orleans black bourgeois. The worship was quiet, and supported by a sanctuary choir who sang the great 16th century church anthems, while hearing a well-ordered homily from Pastor Nicholas Hood. We thought we had found a church that satisfied our longing for growth, only to find that our search was a journey in search of our identity. Our search came to an end, and we returned to New Zion longing for what we were familiar with; the people, the way of life of the people, the Afro centricity of the black Baptist experience. We remained active members of New Zion until I relocated to Chicago, Illinois. I moved to Chicago in 1959, and followed the dictates of the Baptist Covenant which states that, "When we remove from this place, we engage as soon as possible to unite with some other church where we can carry out the spirit of this covenant and the principles of God's word." I joined the Greater Bethesda Missionary Baptist Church, under the pastorate of Reverend Doctor A. Lincoln James, Sr. Bethesda was a large literate Black congregation which encouraged education, instituted various enlightened ministries, and a refined music department. It was not the typical black Baptist church as there were large numbers of professional persons among its membership. Gospel music was not regularly programmed, however, the singing of Negro Spirituals were a constant reminder of black heritage. Many of those who attended Bethesda had an air of accomplishment about them, they saw themselves as the ones who had made it to fairer economics.

Up to this point, I felt that I was a part of the church, because, by my parents' expectations, church brought balance to life, and especially to those of us who were not a factor in the overall American social order. Earlier in this book I mentioned that I left the protestant faith, and entered the Catholic Church, and all because I had a strong need for spiritual nurture while hospitalized which did not come to me from my immediate pastor, but from a Catholic priest. When I was released from the hospital I aligned myself with Saint Dorothy's Catholic Church, received instructions, and was baptized into the Catholic tradition. After two years, I relocated to another neighborhood, and became a member of Saint Francis De Paula Catholic Church.

I struggled with my spiritual development to the point that I felt that I had no need for the church any longer in my life, and so I found many reasons to cease attending, and replaced church with my social agenda. I sang in nightclubs, smoked cigarettes, caroused with illegitimate persons, mismanaged my resources, and drank alcohol. I moved to Washington, D.C. in 1967, and after marriage, when our first child was born, church became part of my life again. I felt like a prodigal, after having wandered for years participating in alien behavior. I needed a ground of Godly faith, and a reprioritization of values. We, as a family began attending Christ United Methodist Church in Southwest Washington, until our move to Alexandria, Virginia, where I returned to the Baptist Church, and was eventually licensed to preach, and ordained at the Alfred Street Baptist Church.

I found my place in the church as an ordained minister of the Gospel, and served faithfully. It seems that God had been preparing me for this great work all the days of my life, even when I was searching in and out of church. My talents for speaking and singing became an asset to my ministry. The years I spent as an administrator in the government provided me with knowledge of how to manage people, and my years of organizational experience with Martin Luther King, Jr. gave me insight into resolving social issues by using the Social Gospel approach. I consistently thank God for my blessed marriage, and family. Again, my marriage is God's answer to my many years of devout prayers.

Since I gave my life to the service of God, I have labored under the impression that many unexplained things in life would become crystal clear, and that life would be uncomplicated by mere obedience to God, but my impression has been clouded by my naive understanding of the trials, toils and tribulations of Jesus Himself during his trek to Calvary, and human suffering by many for righteousness sake. Albert Nolan, in his treatise, regarding the Role of Suffering and Death, writes about the Jews in Maccabean times, and the Zealots, in Jesus' time when they died as martyrs on account of their righteousness.[1] The church has been at the forefront of discussions, because of its positive action, and rightful place at the juncture of good and evil, but the church has also been part of the same discussion, because of its inaction in the lives of men and women who need a voice in a turbulent wilderness of wicked behavior. I have come to believe and accept that the church, which Jesus established upon Saint Peter, is the institution that is to be the inevitable victor of righteousness. Let the church be the church that Jesus founded.

I believe further that black American life finds its foundation in the institution of the church. Outside of the immediate family, the church is where we developed our first interpersonal relationships. It was also the place where we learned Christian virtues, and the commands for living in peace with others. The black church experience contributes to many developed talents in music, speaking, organization, leadership, and cooperation. The church has evolved based on its foundation on the principles of Jesus Christ. It is important to provide a bit of the historical background on the church that was established by Jesus Christ. The Holy Bible provides some enlightenment on the earthly establishment of the church at Caesarea Philippi, a pagan city known for its worship of many Greek gods. It was important in the growth of the disciples to know for themselves who Jesus really was. In his questions, "whom do men say that I am," and more precisely, "whom do you say that I am," The latter question confronts us with the journey of Christianity. Until we know who Jesus Christ is, we are chasing an undefined cause, which fades into oblivion during times of peril. Some of the disciples responded that Jesus was John the Baptist, Elias, Jeremiah or one of the prophets. His second question became even more critical. The time had come for Peter to rise to the occasion of an emphatic announcement, as he said, "thou are the Christ!" Recognizing that only God revealed such an answer to Peter, Jesus responded that "You, Peter, are a stone, and upon this rock I will build my church, and all the powers of hell shall not prevail against it."

Jesus established His church for the purpose of providing humanity with a community of the faithful in maintaining relationships. Man has deviated on to a collision path to meet doom head-on. We have come a very long way from Caesarea Philippi, and have taken a path that appears to be more comfortable, but in fact is fraught with the vicissitudes of a complexed life that need not be. Many of the churches today resemble the church that Jesus established and their behavioral modes are practiced, such as the raising of holy hands, affirmation responses to the preacher, the singing of hymns, and physical ecstasy in the form of shouting. Much of this is authentic Afro-centric in nature, but has the appearance of dramatical entertainment, and profitable business. The author's observations are no indictment of people who have a true experience in the Holy Spirit. The need for a sound spiritual foundation based on unconditional faith is paramount in negotiating the perils and pitfalls of society. In days past, the practiced teachings of the church were a stabilizing influence on our life's journey, and to some degree that is still the case. However, there appears to be a marked modification of the institutional church as it was established.

I have had an opportunity to submerge myself in the workings of many churches, where I discovered a void in the basic understanding of the demonstrated life of Jesus Christ. Authentic Christian teaching and practice is the very core of positive societal change. We are living in a time period when mainline churches are attended as places of status and business connections. Church programs, "ministries" are geared to attract attendance of those who have the potential to swell the financial coffers.

Preachers often do not teach God's word in context, and gimmicks that sustain the competing interest of the world often influence their preaching. Building on centuries of past church helping experiences, the Civil Rights Movement of the 1960s found its resource base in the church. The church doors were open when the world was closed to human needs, and it was the one place that was a sanctuary that addressed most needs of black people. The church was a safe harbor until the Klu Klux Klan, and other hate mongers decided that black empowerment is created and harbored in the black church, thus, the fire bombings. We now have a strong need to revisit the wisdom of the church serving as a place of refuge from the cruelties of the world.

When I first became a minister, I was open to learning all I could about the work of clergy. I enrolled in special seminary classes, attended church conventions, and associations, joined clerical organizations, and became ensconced in clerical matters of ministry. While there are numerous exceptions, I was appalled at the unsavory behavior and decorum of many pastors who are expected to be positive community examples and were looked to as moral and spiritual models for the community. While attending some conventions, I observed ministers who grouped with those who seemed to occupy high places, those who were successful preachers with large followings. They were seekers of worldly riches, and false dreams. The consumption of alcoholic beverages, revival hustlers, and church politics became the order of the day at the weeklong conventions. In an effort to impress onlookers, they drove their state of the art Lincoln Town Cars, Cadillacs, Mercedes, Jaguars and Lexi. This was to make a statement of success. Our communities need moral leaders who understand the spartan life of Jesus, and what his sacrifice means to the world. If those who have set themselves up as Christian leaders understood the essence of the work of Jesus, they would want to emulate a spiritual life that was called to induce hope in a world of the poor, the blind, the lame, the crippled, the lepers, the hungry, the miserable and the least of humankind.

My journey has opened my eyes to the need of the church to spend more time teaching and living the gospel than in celebration, which comes once the truth is known. I make no false pronouncements of sanctity for myself of unblemished righteousness, for I live in a world that is contagious with the germ of iniquity. However, it is my intent and desire to continue on the path of "becoming," while being fully cognizant of the fact that I am imperfect at best. I remain in process of attempting to do good and avoid evil. If I were free of sin, I would not need God. The church, is the one institution where like minds and spirits can ban together and create a community of positive hopes and dreams that makes manifest the presence of God's work at making the world a better place to live. It appears that as we move closer to prosperity, we have less time for the church. Tennis courts, golf courses, boating harbors, brunches, football games, places of leisure all appear to have a larger drawing card of persons during the hours of worship than the church. We have gradually become estranged from the church. As an ordained minister of the gospel according to Jesus Christ, I see the church is losing its attraction for those who struggle with the everyday rigors of their lives. People cannot relate to faith and patience, unless they see it being made manifest in those who profess to have such faith. The words, "I would rather see a sermon lived than preached" are the words that were given me by my mother at the beginning of my ministry. Far too many, so called ministers, live such lives of hypocrisy, and lack the in-depth understanding and practice of the bible. They contribute more to confusion than spiritual growth.

Churches appear to be in competition with other churches for larger congregations, oversized edifices, and financial collections. No church has any business living in opulence, especially when there are such large numbers of the poor among us. If we truly believe the lyrics to the hymn, "God Will Take Care of You," why do we store today and assume that God will not provide tomorrow? I call every church that professes its faith in Almighty God to surrender the mind set and trappings of the world, and put your complete trust in Him, and you will find that tomorrow belongs to Him also.

The church is the one foundational institution in the community of faith where all issues of life can be met and resolved. The company of other believers is an interconnected joy that provides covenanted comfort to the weary isolated traveler on life's lonely path. If the churches were in communion together, there would be no power outside of it that could weaken its strength. If churches worked collaboratively, poverty could be obliterated, inadequate education could be made adequate, affordable housing could be made a reality, families could be strengthened, relationships across racial and cultural relations could be made positive, and peace could be the order of the time. However, when each church operates as a fiefdom, we have more to understand about Jesus' proclamation to Peter upon whom He established His church.

Let the church be the church that it was during my service in the Civil Rights Movement of the 1960s. During that time our churches became havens for spiritual and community initiatives. Prior to the time that Rosa Parks sat down in the white section of a public transit bus in Montgomery, Alabama, the local churches were separate entities, and did little to amalgamate their common interest. Rosa Parks' refusal to accept and participate in a segregated system caused churches to bond and demonstrate a power that had not been realized before. It was the vision of Dr. Martin Luther King, Jr. who called the church to its rightful position of leadership to inform and address the social order of its ills, and proposed a lasting remedy for moral and spiritual order. In my many years of Christian ministry, I have grown to understand the role of the church in a divided world that is destined toward change.

The French political scientist, Alexis de Tocqueville, observed the church that is caught up in a runaway selfish society. He experienced an innumerable multitude of men, all equal and alike, incessantly endeavoring to procure the petty and paltry pleasures with which they glut their lives. Each of them, living apart, is as a stranger to the fate of all the rest; his children and his private friends constitute to him the whole of mankind. As for the rest of his fellow citizens, he is close to them, but he does not see them; he touches them, but he does not feel them; he exists only in himself and for himself alone....[2]

I am persuaded that the leadership of the church must move from the state of self-interest to a broader spectrum of selflessness, in carrying out the true meaning of Jesus' inclusive intent for the church. I suppose one can make a case for selfish behavior. During the 1960s the architects and strategists of the Civil Rights Movement used self-interest to an advantage, but the basic nature and behavior of the participants underwent no real positive modification other than some legislative actions. Morality is not legislatively negotiable. Dennis A. Jacobson, in his book, "Doing Justice," points out how self-interest was used during this period. *"The self interest of the African American community was clear. Thousands were prepared to go to jail, and some were willing to face even death in order to secure basic human rights. Northern liberal politicians wanted to get elected. Businesspeople wanted to protect their economic investments. Government could not endure ongoing, massive social unrest. The media had gripping, valuable stories to broadcast..."*[3] The late Mayor Richard J. Daley dramatically demonstrated the self-interest of the Chicago leadership by reversing police brutality to the demonstrators to overly protecting the demonstrators as the result of worldwide criticism. When we think of selflessness, we focus on those who are position themselves in obscure and practice self-denial. The church elected to follow the path of selflessness, as understood from the life of Jesus.

When the church becomes the church, creature suffering and need can be diminished, and less dependence on the secular world. When the church becomes the church, human racial and cultural relationships become connected, leaving no room for bigotry, segregation, racism or stereotyping. In the words John Oxenham's great hymn of the church: *In Christ there is no East or West, in him no South or North, but one great fellowship of love Thru-out the whole wide earth.*

CHAPTER XVI

RACE AND CULTURE

Part of the dream that was held by the late Reverend Doctor Martin Luther King, Jr. in his dramatic address from a podium at the Lincoln Memorial on 28, August 1963, was that the sons of former slaves and sons of former slave owners would be able to sit down together at the table of brotherhood, and that his four little children would one day live in a nation where they would not be judged by the color of their skin but by the content of their character. black persons all over America related to this proclamation with great hope that such an aura would sweep our beloved country. Today, we still live apart in every aspect of life, when it comes to race and culture. We have not been able to reconcile the fact that we are not that much unalike. The same laws of nature bind us, however, we find great difficulty filling the void that divides us. During my lifetime I have never been allowed to put aside racial differences, and feel the full acceptance as a man. When I enter a room of white persons, my first thought is whether I will be accepted equally among them, or if my presence counts for anything.

My very first experience of racial integration was, in 1957 during my college days at Xavier. A Catholic priest by the name of Francis Berkely served as music director at Saint Patrick's Catholic Church. Saint Patrick's was without a choir for the various masses that were offered. Father Berkley had an idea of organizing a special choir by using paid volunteer singers from three of New

Orleans' universities, Loyola, Dillard, and Xavier. During those days, white students attended Loyola, and Dillard and Xavier were two black universities. The choir was formed and sang for two masses each Sunday, and for special Holy days. Messrs David Butolph and Robert Rohe served as interchangeable directors. These were two white men from Dillard University, and the New Orleans Philharmonic Symphony. As a student of Xavier, I had grown accustomed to having white teachers, but I had never experienced racial integration beyond the boundaries of the campus. Racial integration was prohibited and punishable by law throughout the south, and New Orleans was no exception. One evening, after choir rehearsal, Father Berkley invited the choir to the rectory for wine and cheese, with full knowledge of the laws against race mixing, I was reluctant to attend, but was encouraged. This was my first introduction to social racial integration. Here I found that we had much in common, and the only issue at hand was the stupid laws that divided us. I could not wait to get home to tell my mother that I had participated in my first social racial integration event. The experience with white students in the choir and other social events provided me with a broader view of humanity, and how relationships are built from common interests.

Many years have passed since 1957, and racism continues to surface in all venues of American life, and especially in the areas of education, employment, and housing. Equitable treatment for minorities and civil rights has not been nor is it high on the agenda of those issues that are important to America. The 21st century has ushered into America new population of third world immigrants who are made up of different cultures, thereby creating different dynamics in the normal flow of American life. We are now undergoing a basic change in human relations in our neighborhoods, places of public assembly, ecclesiastical institutions, schools, and places of employment. We need the vision of a new world order where the respect of human diversity is honored and celebrated. My racially segregated life has had the opposite affect on my life; it has strengthened my determination and given me a resolve to continue my trek to the goal of freedom for those who know it not. In the course of human events, I believe in the righteousness of the divine order of an unseen God who dispenses justice in times of great peril. In the case of unequal justice among the races of men, the oppressed continue to ask the question of the prophet Amos, "When will judgment run down as waters, and righteousness as a mighty stream?" The answer comes from an unconditional faith, and the unrelenting devotion to sacrifice. Only this combination will create a world in which all can thrive.

My life is given to indulging my being in bringing about peaceful coexistence in the human family of man. In addition to my earlier work and commitment to Civil Rights, the untiring work in the field of Human Relations, at home and abroad, the time spent in attempting to instill wholeness in those who are wards of the penal systems, I have organized and established a human relations corporation as an answer to the need for improved understanding between races and cultures across the American community. The corporation is called REACH, Incorporated, Racial Equality and Cultural Harmony. The intent of REACH, Inc. is to facilitate dialogue sessions between racially and culturally diverse groups in a controlled environment. This special work provides opportunities for meaningful and civil exchange between different races and cultures in attempting to resolve their differences. I have combined my rich life's experiences and established forums for diverse groups to peacefully confront their human biases in the workplace, corporate America, educational institutions, and in places of worshipful assembly.

The purpose of REACH is rooted in people of goodwill working together on their differences in an effort to close the divides that keep us apart. The goal is to expose and sensitize participants to the rapidly changing demographics in our society, and to diverse methods of positive behavior to cope with persons who appear to be unlike themselves. Further, the goals encompass enhancing communications across racial and cultural lines; examining the current state of race and cultural relations; developing methods to identify and resolve problems in such critical areas as discrimination, prejudice, and stereotyping; and developing strategies and programs to ensure safer communities, places of employment, schools, and places of public assembly. REACH is a common sense approach to harmonious living in a complex society. While much of REACH is aimed at the adult population, we find that our youth struggle with the same societal issues that perplex adults. In an effort to provide a comfort zone for youth to air their differences in a non-threatening environment, I added a special feature to REACH called "THE STUDENT CONNECTION," which is a special program for middle and high school youth who are interested in working toward a better understanding of the different races and cultures in their community. The Student Connection is an initiative that responds to the need to enhance better communications between students of different races and cultures. I established this bold attempt to have participants to do an introspective review of their view of the worlds in which they live, with hopes of effecting positive change in behavioral practices. It is noteworthy to observe that our youth are more honest about their feelings, and have no reticence about expressing them than the adults. I am certain that our future existence is in the hands of our youth, and in their innocence we will overcome someday.

There are numerous groups throughout America working on race and culture relations, and who recognize that the common forces that energize humanity inextricably connect our future. Unfortunately, we have not enjoyed the leadership of dedicated national political or ecclesiastical leaders who have been bold and daring enough to confront this malady of society, except the vision of a great society by the bravery of men like Frederick Douglas, Martin Luther King, Jr., Malcolm X, and other black heroes who have bucked the times with their rhetoric of togetherness.

Slavery was one of the greatest inhumane tragedies that was ever visited on America. It is the active ghosts of slavery, seen and unseen, that will impair our ability to realize our full greatness as we continue to suffer the ravages of that institution of human destruction. Many black people, down through the generations, have not completely realized their inherent equality to white people. As I am persuaded that it will take many more generations to destroy the myth of inequity. Determination is buried in the will of a people to survive at whatever the cost, therefore, freedom and equality come in terms of self-denial, sacrifice, and pride. True freedom will never become a reality to black America until white America is free.

The struggle between races and cultures will forever be an impediment on the road to harmony among humankind, until we come to learn more about each other, and brave the divides that keep us apart. Every culture celebrates their existence and feels that they have a right to be where they choose. If we knew each other better and had the willingness to explore our differences, we could come to a point of positive co-existence. White people suffer their guilt because of past slavery, and black people suffer the degradation by white people. Because of past negative behaviors and practices between races and cultures, human insensitivities are heightened to such a point that stereotyping becomes the order of the time. In some cases we perceive negative things that really aren't, and overlook things that are positive and relevant to our coming together.

When I began my job assignment in the Alexandria City Government, I had great aspirations of making a real positive difference in race relations throughout the government and the city, and I found others who shared my enthusiasm. Much of my readiness for this position was my fundamental faith in the goodwill of most people. My many years of working on the issues of race and culture throughout the U. S. and the world and my commitment to all of the guiding principles of the Office on Human Rights summed up all of the meaningful activities that I had been dedicated to up to this point. My passion for this work was lauded everywhere I served. However, I continue to make the point that until we know one another and have the willingness to explore our differences, we will never close the bothersome gap that keeps us apart. In the words of Martin Luther King, Jr. we must live together as brothers and sisters or perish together as fools." The path of life is encumbered with those who find difficulty in negotiating their existence; therefore I am obligated by God to help them along the way as I pass.

CHAPTER XVII

CONTINUING THE JOURNEY

Up to now my life's journey has been a series of continuous development and new experiences. My nature is goal oriented with calculated risks. I am often reminded of the price for victory. Real victory comes as the result of commitment and dedication to a specific goal. A goal that is not obstructed by my inability to persevere. I have always believed that if what I am going after is worth pursuing, and then nothing should deter or dissuade me from obtaining it.

I learned many years ago in high school, a successful runner is taught to never look back in pursuit of the goal, but to run the race with confidence, thrusting the body forward and pressing on to the goal which is ahead. The goal is the end for which I aim for success.

My life's work is still in its formative stage with much more to be realized. It is my contention that I have achieved nothing that deserves acclaim, because I have not reached my goal. I remain in a state of becoming. I am not there yet.

My goal is involved in the good of humanity with great hope that we will all come to value our racial and cultural diversity, and celebrate together as the family of God. Many people of various cultures and races have sacrificed their lives for the sake of unity among humankind, and still the struggle continues.

I must continue the journey, because we will forever forfeit the true benefits of the gift of life by a caring God. Those who share my passion for a peaceful social order must adhere to the resounding words of the poet, Henry David Thoreau: *If a man does not keep pace with his companions, perhaps it is because he hears a different drummer. Let him step to the music he hears, however measured or faraway.* The drummer that I hear is one of peace and harmony, and that will always be my pursuit

While the writing of America's history appears to have been slanted to exclude those of African extraction, the brilliant penmanship of Thomas Jefferson's drafting of a specific section of the Declaration of Independence, leaves many questions unanswered:

> We hold these truths to be self-evident,
> that all men are created equal, that they
> are endowed by their creator with certain
> unalienable rights, that among these are
> life, liberty and the pursuit of happiness...

History has demonstrated the true meaning of "all men." Isn't it true that black males were not considered men? Were the unalienable rights abridged for black men? If these questions are answered honestly, herein lies the contradiction in the foundation of America History is muddled with misinformation, and has omitted that which was intended by our creator. As a young boy growing up in the antebellum South, I dreamed of freedom and equality only to awaken from the dream to the nightmare of reality inequality and increasing hopelessness. Fortunately, it has been hope that provided me with the strength to persevere through the struggle, and prepares me to continue the journey. It would be gravely misstated if I declared that America has not made some positive changes in race relations. Many persons of color have taken advantage of the opportunities that were unfolded before them. Opportunities are for those who have the courage and qualifications to pursue them without social impediments.

The dark blot of slavery provides us with a sordid past, but we stand at the threshold of another century lauding our accomplishments in these matters of inequity, however, the poet Robert Frost stated, *The woods are lovely, dark and deep but I have promises to keep, and miles to go before I sleep, and miles to go before I sleep.*

When we take into account the progress of America's thriving cities, and boast of the substantial economy and the increasing intellect of many of our citizens, no wonder we feel proud of the world's richest country. Sobering reality calls my attention to the disproportionate representation of black Americans in the U.S. criminal justice system.

Since most inmates are adult black men, they are incarcerated at rates that are twelve to twenty-six times greater than those of white men. Because of their extraordinary rate of incarceration, one in every 20 black men over the age of 18 is in a state or federal prison, compared to one in every 180 whites. All crimes should meet the demands of justice, but there appears to be an imbalance in incarcerated criminals. Marc Mauer's account of some of the reasons for this kind of disparity points to poverty, education, neighborhood of arrest, and indirect discrimination.[1]

Secretary of Education Rod Paige said, "The most egregious issue that must be confronted is the achievement gap between the performance of minority kids and their peers." The January 4, 2004 edition of the Washington Daily Newspaper reported that according to the 2000 National Assessment of Education Progress (NAEP) test, 63 percent of black inner-city fourth graders and 58 percent of urban Hispanic fourth-graders are unable to demonstrate a "basic" proficiency in reading. The major implication being more than four decades after Brown v. Board of Education, our public schools remain unequal.

The above examples of social injustices are a major reason why I must continue the journey of standing up for the disallowed and disavowed. There are many other issues of racial inequity, such as, the affordable housing calamity, that has a bearing on education, crime, employment and the lack of reasonable health assistance programs for indigent people and the elderly.

With ongoing high inflationary cost for goods, it becomes impossible for the unemployed and underemployed to maintain daily subsistence. It becomes all the more important to provide support measures for those who find difficulty in living. I mentioned earlier how important it is for the people of God to assume their rightful role in under-girding those who are less fortunate. We would ordinarily think the people of God are found in the confines of the churches, mosques and synagogues. While some faith institutions have been responsive, much more is needed. I continue to believe there are more people of goodwill than not, however they are much too silent on issues that matter.

As a Baptist minister, I espouse the social gospel approach to Christian service. This approach transforms the written gospel into action. The social gospel is not something that draws its meaning from scripture, but a response to a need in the social order of humankind. Frederick Nymeyer says the social gospel may be defined as proposals for political, social and economic organization of society, based on principles of morality which are considered (1) not to be applicable to individuals, but (2) are applicable to men acting collectively...groups and class relations are considered and not individual relations.[2]

It is my desire to avail myself to opportunities that help people to wholeness with a clear understanding that they learn how to fish and eat daily rather than accepting a fish as charity and eat sometimes. I have a vision to continue to assist prison inmates, men and women, in the positive transformation of their lives from crime to fully contributing citizens. This can only be done when there is openness to change, and a willingness to modify behavioral patterns. At the writing of this book, a small group of inmates at the Alexandria Adult Detention Center, under my guidance, are fully engaged in developing a program for drug users to be treated in lieu of prison. Many inmates are serving time in jails for using drugs when they should be in treatment for their sickness.

The matter of working on preparation for the future through our youth is a vitally important issue. The Student Connection, that is a forum for youth dialogue on race and culture, youth developmental concerns, character development and leadership. This is a proven initiative that has caused positive transformation of behaviors that have stymied progress in youth development. The Student Connection activities result in normal interactive relationships between cultures, in a changing society, and build bridges to connect the divides. Experience teaches us that youth are not reticent about discussing sensitive issues such as race and culture. This program initiative assures a positive community building process

The whole concept of honest community dialogue on issues where disagreements have been barriers can be a great beginning to healing wounds of discord, and to bringing about positive resolves in cementing relationships. America needs to call time out for understanding our differences. I maintain that I am committed to continuing the journey to peace and harmony.

CHAPTER XVIII

FOREVER HOPEFUL

Life without hope for tomorrow is stagnant and lost in the immediacy of the moment. If I arose each day without a desire or expectation of what the unfolding day would bring, my outlook on the future would be like vanishing mist at sunrise. I have hope that humanity will revert to the good that God intended in His divine creation plan. The essence of hope is accompanied by joy, peace, and the will to persevere. Our very existence and accomplishments rest on the foundation of hope in an achievable goal that is seen before it appears.

The fulfillment of hope comes with essential faith as the driving force toward an expected end. Faith is found in confidence and conviction that brings one to a state of being free from doubt thereby providing a spirit of hope. This spirit of hope has been the catapulting vehicle for all who dare to succeed in any given feat. Peter F. Drucker, in his treatise found in the Atlantic Monthly, November 1994, wrote about "The Age of Social Transformation," which provides a sensible argument for hoping for a better world order.[1] His research is predicated on the many social radical transformations that were achieved during the twentieth century. Great progress is founded in the will and hope of a people who are dedicated to improving their lot. Such aspirations are realized when we come to understand the totality of the order of creation. It was God's intent that man would have dominion over the earth, which necessitates visionary outlook in hope for the unseen miracles wrought by God.

I live daily with the hope of humanity growing to appreciate, celebrate, and respect our racial and cultural differences in making this a world of peace and harmony. It is the realization of this hope that will hold the fabric of society together in unity. It becomes beneficial to the effort of unity to analyze the successes and perils of socialization in human history in hopes that we negate the mistakes of the past.

In retrospect, as I reflect on the journey that has brought me to this point, I experience the dichotomy of pride and shame. Pride in my early guided development from my parents and those whom I met along the way; pride in multiple accomplishments in spite of the social climate and impediments that were to encumber my path. The shame is found in this country that has the wherewithal to demonstrate a balanced diverse society for the world to emulate, but chooses to gloat in arrogance and greed in the face of suffering.

I have great hope for America, because I believe there are more people of goodwill than not, however they choose to be silent about the issues that should matter. This hope, also, rests in the demonstrated resilience through the great depression of 1929, and the ability to reign victorious in World Wars One and Two, the willingness to support and aid fledgling foreign countries, and the maintaining of public freedoms that have the potential to some day include all people.

America has always been rooted in hope, even with its internal problems. Until the destruction of the World Trade Center in New York City in the year 2001, the world saw us as the model of freedom and democracy. It is my hope that we regain such respect. We have signaled to others we are a God fearing nation, and our strength comes from our strong hope and faith in overcoming the unpredictable. We claim the nations hope is "In God We Trust," as this inscription is found on the currency we use. It is apparent that Secretary of the Treasury Salomon P. Chase, in 1861, adhered to an appeal for Godly recognition of our nation. Hope is ingrained in the daily life of America in much of our public musical pronouncements, i.e., "God Bless America," "America The Beautiful," "Lift

Every Voice and Sing," and God of Our Fathers." These hopeful pronouncements serve to enhance my determination to continue to press on for justice, righteousness, and freedom for every American to have the right to be free.

There are times when hope is made manifest in public acts of willful civil disobedience, resulting in violence or jail. These rebellious demonstrations become necessary to highlight injustices to the victims of oppression. Without this form of hopeful protest during the 1950s and 1960s, the cause of Civil Rights would have been hopeless. As a participant in such demonstrations, I am not ashamed, because these acts were not only necessary, but also desirable.

Within the past three decades, black Americans have become aroused from their unwanted slumber of rejection to exercise the right to be a part of the mainstream of American life, and this forward activity will not be capitulated, because of minuscule changes. Federal civil rights legislation, and the goodwill of many white people have certainly been positive responses to the multiple wrongs that have been perpetrated against Black people, however my hope is the wheels of righteousness and justice for all people move at a greater velocity.

Again, my hope is built on God's demonstrated care for the down trodden and disenfranchised. Over the past three decades the social progress in America has signaled a ray of hope for systemic social change. Since reconstruction, the latter part of the twentieth century voters sent more black legislators to the U.S. Congress than ever before. In January 1969, Black American representatives of the 77th Congress formed the Democratic Select Committee." The Committee changed its name to the Congressional Black Caucus formed in 1971. The founding members were made up of Shirley Chisholm, William Gray, George Collins, John Conyers, Ronald Dellums, Charles Diggs, Augustus Hawkins, Ralph Metcalf, Peririn Mitchell, Robert Nix, Charles Rangel, Louise Stokes, and D C Delegate Walter Fauntroy.

They established goals that were to influence events that concern black Americans, and to achieve more equity for persons of African descent. My work with the Urban Coalition, during this period, was to assist in setting the national agenda for the Black

Caucus, while traveling the country seeking issues from black America that would be of concern to the Caucus. I remain proud of the modicum of progress that has been made with the understanding that hope for better days are inevitable.

Finally, my hope is vested in the words of the late Martin Luther King, Jr., as found in his essay, "A Testament of Hope:"

> *"A voice out of Bethlehem two thousand years ago said that all men are created equal. It said right would triumph. Jesus of Nazareth wrote no books; he owned no property to endow him with influence. He had no friends in the courts of the powerful. But he changed the course of mankind with only the poor and despised. Naïve and unsophisticated though we may be, the poor and despised of the twentieth century will revolutionize this era. In our "arrogance, lawlessness and gratitude, "we will fight for human justice, brotherhood, secure peace and abundance for all. When we have won these—in a spirit of unshakable nonviolence—-then, in luminous splendor, the Christian era will truly begin."*

It is with this hope that my journey will be fulfilled, and my path will continue to be intersected by those who desire the day of righteousness for all of God's people, because I will not pass this way again.

EPILOGUE

From obscurity to a level place in life can be recited by many, the road has been said to be tolerable or difficult to travel, however, difficulties have caused many persons to give up the journey to failure or the lack of endurance. Those who began their lives at a level place are confronted with a multiple of choices not unlike those who are less fortunate. The created intent of human interacting relationships is vital in searching for success. In a world of differing ideals, philosophies and Theologies solid and meaningful relationships are sometimes hard to come by. When a good connection happens, it is wise to cherish it and nurture the bond in the hopes of growing, learning, and sharing. My life has been enriched many times over from the many good relationships that I have had with diverse humanity from all over the world in my quest for the true meaning of my existence. To live life is tantamount to an excursion taken by any mode of transportation that one chooses. The one time life journey can be smooth, turbulent or crash prone, depending on your goal and the route that you chose to travel. Recognizing that I have one chance at the fulfillment of my life, it has been important that I sought out and surrounded myself with a talented resource pool of relationships who have enhanced my life, and enabled me to share with those I meet as I continue this journey. I have often stated that the best made plans can go awry when divine order intercepts your life. I thought that I knew what I wanted my life to be. I thought it out and began to operate in the niche that I had carved out for myself. I was planning to be one of the world's accomplished vocal artist, after all, I was born with a divine gift of a melodic baritone voice accompanied by some of the most talented music teachers and coaches in the field. My work in concert singing has never amounted to very much, because of many adverse variables in the concert world and my own waning interest. We are all born with many talents in reserve. Often we don't dig deep enough into the crevices of our being to discover our other selves.

I have the firm belief that we were not created to be limited in our lives but to live a full interactive life of service until we are no more. The realization of positive human relationships is made manifest when we become our brother's keeper in the real sense of being a good neighbor. So, the world has been set before us for our growth and development, but not entirely unto us alone, but to the whole of human creation for a more harmonious diverse world order. While we pass this way, give everything you have to love, peace, and harmony, regardless of race or culture, because we will not pass this way again.

ENDNOTES

PREFACE

[1] John Donne, Devotions Upon Emergent Occasions, Meditations XVII. The Anglican Library, 2000.

[2] Major General John Stanford, U.S. Army (Ret), Victory in Our Schools, New York. Bantam Books, 1999.

Chapter I

[1] Chester Morgan, Redneck Liberal: Theodore Gilmore Bilbo and The New Deal. Baton Rouge, 1995.

[2] Adam Nossiter, Of Long Memory. Cambridge, Da Capo Press, Cambridge, MA. 1994.

Chapter II

[1] A Testament of Hope, ed. James M. Washington (Harper and Row, San Francisco, 1986).

[2] Martin Luther King, Jr., Stride Toward Freedom. Harper and Row, San Francisco. 1958.

[3] Charles V. Hamilton, Adam Clayton Powell. Collier Books, New York, 1991.

Chapter III

[1] Saint Katharine Drexel, Benefactress to the Needs of Native Americans and African Americans. She was the founder of many schools for the needy including Xavier University of New Orleans, Louisiana.

Chapter XII

[1] Anais Nin, The Diary of Anais Nin, Harcourt Brace Jovanovich, Inc, New York: 1969. p. 307.

Chapter XV

[1] Albert Nolan, Jesus Before Christianity. Orbis Books, Maryknoll, NY: 2001.

[2] Alexis de Tocqueville, Democracy in America. Ed. J. P. Mayer. Trans. George Lawrence. New York: Anchor, 1969.

[3] Dennis A. Jacobson, Doing Justice. Fortress Press, Minneapolis, MN. 2001.

Chapter XVII

[1] Marc Mauer, Race to Incarcerate (New York: The New Press, 1999) pp. 118-142.

[2] Frederick Nymeyer, What Is The Social Gospel? Progressive Calvinism, 1957.

Chapter XVIII

[1] Peter F. Drucker, The Age of Social Transformation, The Atlantic Monthly, November 1994.